SOFT Cheese CRAFT

For Paul

SOFT Cheese CRAFT

and other RECIPES for the ASPIRING dairymaid

by MARY ANN PIKE

WHITTET BOOKS

First published 1982

Whittet Books Ltd, The Oil Mills, Weybridge, Surrey

Design by Richard Adams

British Library Cataloguing in Publication Data
Pike, Mary Ann
Soft cheese craft.
1. Cheese
I. Title
637'.352 SF271
ISBN 0-905483-24-3

Acknowledgments

The author is indebted to the following individuals for their assistance with the compilation of this book: Ann Truman and Mrs S. Hayes of the National Dairy Council; Joy Ellery, Milk Marketing Board; G.G. Hand, A.L.A., and Miss A.E.E. McDougle, F.L.A., of North Yorkshire County Libraries; R. Jakes, County of Cambridgeshire Library; Paxton & Whitfield; Dr Sadie B. Ward, Institute of Agricultural History and Museum of Rural Life; Fred and Emily Manning and Mrs S. Humber.

The author would like to thank the following for permission to quote from copyright material: Peterborough (M. Green), *Daily Telegraph*; Macmillan and David Garnett for an extract from *The Master Cat*; Routledge and Kegan Paul Ltd and Val Cheke for an extract from *The Story of Cheesemaking in Britain*; Bruce H. Axler for an extract from *The Cheese Handbook*; W. Foulsham & Co. Ltd for an extract from *Old English Cookery* by Peggy Hutchinson.

The pictures on the following pages are reproduced by kind permission of the Museum of English Rural Life, University of Reading: 11, 24, 34, 56 (2), 62–3, 64, 74, 82–3, 88, 106–7.

Typeset by Inforum Ltd, Portsmouth
Printed and bound in Great Britain at The Pitman Press, Bath

Contents

1

The Dairy-Maid's Duties
1872

'Punctuality, order, and cleanliness must be observed in all dairy work.

'The dairy-maid should be an early riser, for, in the summer months especially, much of her work will have to be done before breakfast. In preparing the dairy for use the walls must be whitewashed, the windows cleaned, and the shelves scrubbed with cold water and a brush kept for that purpose, and never used for the dairy utensils, and the floor nicely cleaned. Having heated the copper she must next take her best scrub-brush and thoroughly scour every part of the dairy utensils with cold water, rinsing them well, and if they are to be used for milk, cream, butter, curd or cheese, afterwards scalding them and placing them in the rack and on shelves conveniently for use, taking care to keep "a place for everything and everything in its place". The milk pans (earthenware preferred) may be piled in a stack and taken down as wanted.

'Fuller's earth or wood ashes are sometimes used for scouring with cold water, but soap must never be used, for it would surely spoil the cream and butter.

'Should the herdsman milk the cows, it is necessary to see

that they are milked perfectly dry, as the richest part comes last, and the dairy-maid should be particular to have her clean pans ready to receive the milk, which must be set or emptied into them at once. Next she should rinse the pail with cold water, scalded, and hung to dry. This must be done once a day. In the evening rinse the pail with cold water and wipe it with the dairy cloth. If either the pail or cloth were neglected, it would spoil all the cream and butter.

'After the milk has been standing twenty-four hours, the dairy-maid will take a skimmer and basin with a spout and proceed to skim the cream off, first loosening it round the edge with her finger. Then put in the skimmer and take up as much cream as it will hold, allowing the milk to drain off before putting it into the basin. This is repeated until all the cream has been carefully removed. As the small basin is filled, it is transferred from time to time to the cream-pot, into which a piece of saltpetre, about the size of a nut, is dropped with the first lot of cream only, and stirred with a flat wooden stick, which is left in, as it will be required to stir the cream every time any is added. Should the cream be more than three days for butter-making, it should be put into another clean pot and stirred daily as before. This process gives it ventilation and keeps it better.

'The skim milk may be used for domestic purposes, bread making, puddings, etc., and the remainder (if not sold) may be given to the calves, pigs, and poultry with advantage.

'After the milk pans have been emptied, they should at once be carefully washed with the scrub-brush and cold water (hot would only set the grease) and well rinsed and dried, and then put away till churning day, when they can be thoroughly done with the rest of the things, as they must be properly scalded before being used again. There are many varieties of churns, such as the barrel, box, air. The latter is the most difficult to use, as it requires the milk to be at a certain temperature, and if either hotter or colder the butter will not come. The American box churn, sold by Messrs. Burgess and Keys, is here recommended as easy to use and easy to clean.'

Extracted from *The Modern Householder*, edited and compiled by Ross Murray (1872)

CHEESE

The Basic Procedure

'They make cheesemongers and pastrycooks knights.'
Goldsmith (1760)

The art of making cheeses is much simpler than most people imagine, and, once the basic science is grasped, cheese-making can prove a fascinating diversion. Cheeses can belong to one of three classes – soft, semi-hard or hard – but this is a very loose classification. At one end of the table there is the soft cheese, which has a very high moisture content (50–80 per cent) and has to be eaten fresh, and at the other end there is the hardened relative, which has been subjected to heavy weighting, to expel as much whey as possible, and which can be matured for years, e.g. Parmesan with a moisture content of 28 per cent. This book deals with the varieties of cheeses that are generally recognized as soft or semi-hard, and, further, that require no specialized equipment to produce them. The only essential item which might not be found in every kitchen is a thermometer. It really is false economy to dabble in cheese-making without one, as the craft is based on timings, temperatures and methods as opposed to varying ingredients – all cheese being basically milk! Muslin is used a lot, but a boiled (i.e. sterilized) tea-towel will do.

Milk

'Milk . . . is a Compound Body of Cream, Cruds, and Whey.'
Bacon in *Sylva sylvarum* (1626)

All cheese is made from milk that has been separated into curds and whey. If raw, unpasteurized milk is left to its own devices it will sour. In effect, the natural bacteria in the raw milk reproduce, raising the acidity of the milk and causing a sour taste. This natural process can be hastened by subjecting the milk to gentle warmth. Obversely, strong heat has the opposite effect. Milk undergoing pasteurization is heated to 161°F/71.7°C (minimum temperature by law) and held at that temperature for at least 15 seconds. This process kills off all the undesirable, disease-harbouring bacteria and renders the milk safe for consumption. Unfortunately, this also destroys most, but not all, of the lactic-acid-producing bacteria that cause the milk to sour. Whilst this does of course improve the keeping qualities of the milk, it does mean that cheese made from pasteurized milk will not be able to develop such a good flavour.

Hence, in order to replace some of the beneficial bacteria – or, in other words, to re-introduce the milk's ability to sour – a starter is added. This is actually a culture of lactic-acid-producing bacteria and is used by cheese manufacturers. It is possible to buy starters but they are expensive. Although there is no harm in buying a commercial starter if you wish, it does seem an unnecessary extravagance for the home cheese-maker when either natural yoghurt or cultured buttermilk can produce very similar results. Both these aliments are readily available and add the pleasant sourness associated with many cheeses. However, if you ever decide to progress to more adventurous cheeses – the ones that flaunt curious holes and fancy moulds and veining – the correct commercial starter is of course a necessity. If unavailable, in the case of a foreign cheese such as Camembert, it is possible to make your own specialized starter from a piece of shop-bought cheese. The procedure is explained in due course in this book. We assume throughout the book that you'll be using pasteurized milk.

Soured milk, whether it is unpasteurized milk that has been

left to sour naturally, or pasteurized milk that has had a starter introduced to it, separates when it attains a certain level of acidity, thus becoming curds and whey. If the whey is drained off, you have curd cheese – it is that simple.

Rennet

'As quickly as the milk is turn'd to curd,
When with a proper rennet it is mixt.'
Hobbes in *Homer's Iliads* (1675)

Of course, all cheese-making is not quite so elementary as the curd cheese formed by high acidity. For a start, it is not desirable for all cheese to have such a pronounced sour taste and so rennet is added to cause the milk to coagulate – or clot – while it still has a low acidity. The most commonly used rennet is a solution made from the lining of the fourth stomach of an unweaned calf. In the animal, the same substance helps the young creature to digest and solidify its first food. A rather hackneyed legend claims that the first cheese was accidentally made when some tribesman found that milk he had stored in a vessel made from an animal's stomach had solidified!

In bygone days, the preparation of rennet for cheese-making was a messy and none too delightful business – one I shall not worry you about – but, happily, to-day we can buy little bottles of rennet, with several kinds available. Junket rennet (or tablets even) can be used for some cheeses when a very soft curd is acceptable. However, for most cheeses, this is simply not strong enough and a proper cheese rennet must be acquired if cheese-like cheeses are going to materialize. As well as the normal cheese rennet, there is also a vegetarian cheese rennet, made from microbial fermentation. This is available from most health food shops and gives excellent results.

The bottled stuff aside, it is also possible to use the enzymes from a number of plants to coagulate milk. In the 16th century one chronicler recorded that the milky sap of 'the Figge tree' would serve as a rennet to make cheese, and the juices from Lady's Bedstraw (*Galium verum* for Latin lovers) have been praised for their milk-clotting powers by countryfolk for many centuries. In Portugal, a wild thistle is used to make *requeijão* – an exceptionally pleasant soft curd cheese, traditionally wrapped in cabbage leaves to keep it moist.

Curds and Whey

'Little Miss Muffet sat on a tuffet, eating her curds and whey.'
Traditional nursery rhyme

Once coagulated, the firm curd can be treated in a variety of different ways according to the kind of cheese to be made. Primarily, the curd is cut or broken – to make curds and whey – and the whey (which consists mainly of water and lactose) is released. The size of the broken curds regulates the speed at which the whey is expelled, and this in turn helps to determine the type of cheese that will finally emerge. Broadly speaking, the smaller the curds, the quicker the drainage and the harder the cheese. Correspondingly, for most soft cheeses, the curds are kept relatively large and the drainage is quite slow.

If the whey is very cloudy, this means that a considerable amount of fat is being lost. This will happen if the curd is treated roughly. Alternatively, it can indicate that the curd has been cut before it has set properly – be it a soft or very firm curd. When ready for cutting, a curd should split cleanly when pressed with a finger. The curds are drained in a number of varying receptacles – in moulds, tin rings or baskets even – according to each recipe, and, when as dry as desired, are salted to taste and stored in a cool place until they are consumed. The next stage, in the more complicated recipes, calls for the curds to be scalded.

Time and Temperature

If you leave milk to sour for longer than the time specified in a recipe, it is possible that you will completely alter the final character of the cheese – not of course that exact, stereotype rules need worry the home cheese-maker, who is probably keen to experiment anyway! But this factor does indicate the importance of both time and temperature in cheesecraft. Heat, for instance, encourages both milk to sour and rennet to coagulate the milk, but too high a heat will prevent rennet from working.

Milk contains soluble calcium, and, once it is heated beyond a certain temperature, this chemical element becomes insoluble. The action is not reversed when the milk is cooled again, and this explains why neither sterilized nor UHT milk (both of which are subjected to a much higher temperature than pasteurized milk) cannot be successfully used in cheese-making when rennet is employed. However, they are both ideal for making yoghurt – and subsequently yoghurt cheese – as before milk is introduced to a yoghurt culture, it should be boiled for several minutes to destroy any bacteria that will otherwise contaminate, and thus spoil, the yoghurt bacteria. (The pasteurization of milk, remember, does not kill all the bacteria in milk.) The boiled milk does of course have to be cooled to a specific temperature, before the yoghurt culture is added, otherwise that too would be killed off!

Hence a thermometer is essential for any constant success with cheese-making – or yoghurt-making for that matter. A floating dairy one is best, but a sugar syrup one, as used for making fondants and the like, will suffice. A room thermometer is also recommended. Ideally the temperature of your dairy – even if it is a kitchen in a suburban semi – should be kept constant around 65° F/18° C. Too high a temperature will cause over-rapid drainage of the curds, and one too low will slow the expulsion of the whey and invite too much acid to develop. But when cheeses are put to ripen or mature, they need a much cooler environment.

As previously mentioned, some cheeses call for the curds to be re-heated or scalded – some authorities even maintain that milk cannot be classified as real cheese unless this process has been effected. The process helps release the whey by shrinking the curd, and all hard cheese has to undergo this operation.

Making the Cheese

Pressing

'The cleanly cheese-press she could never turn.'
John Gay in *The shepherd's week, in six pastorals* (1714)

Some cheeses need to be pressed so yet more whey can be squeezed out and a harder substance formed. However, as this book deals mainly with the softer varieties, this operation is only met once or twice, and the weights are very light. Thus, although useful, a cheese press is not really needed for the recipes in this collection.

Doing the Presswork

Avoiding Contamination

'No caterpillars nor grubs, except the maggot of the small cheese fly . . . can jump . . .'
John Baxter in *Library of Practical Agriculture* (1846)

One last vital note that applies to all kinds of cheese-making – and butter- and yoghurt-making for that matter. All utensils and cloths used should be spotlessly clean, as milk is very easily contaminated. Scalding seems the most practical way to ensure thorough cleanliness – detergents and sterilizing solutions should be used with great care, and the items well rinsed afterwards to eliminate the risk of soapy-tasting cheese. Likewise, neither the making nor storage of cheese should be done anywhere near onions, soap, spices or other strong smellers. And do check for maggots of cheese flies and cheese mites (which look like dust on the cheese), in the ripening stages. If you see any particles or dust which could be tiny eggs, cut them out straight away!

ACID CURD CHEESES

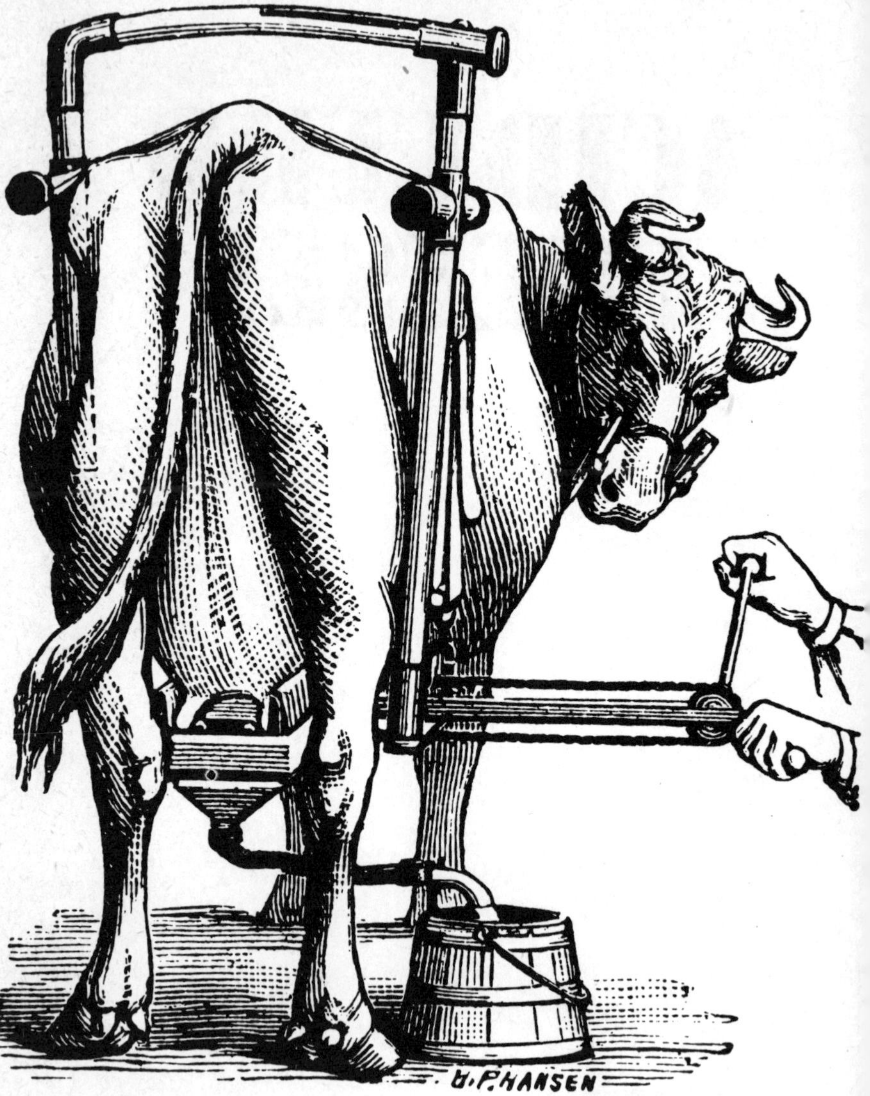
H.P. HANSEN

Lemon Juice Curd Cheese

'This acid . . . transforms the milk into a curd.'
John Baxter (1846)

A very simple curd cheese with a fairly distinctive, but not unpleasant, lemony tang. Not even a thermometer is needed.

To make 8 oz. (225 g.) or 12 oz. (337 g.)
2 or 3 pints (1.120 or 1.680 lit.) milk
2 or 3 tbs. fresh lemon juice
salt to taste

Put the milk in a pan and bring to the boil. Stir in the lemon juice – it should curdle immediately and will not look all that pleasant! Leave aside for 5 minutes or so, and then pour into a fine sieve, or else into a colander, lined with a square of scalded muslin and balanced over a bowl. Leave to drain for another 5 or 10 minutes – obviously, the longer you leave it, the drier the cheese will be (and the less it will weigh!) Mix in a little salt to taste. Scrape the curds into a tub and store in the refrigerator. Eat within a few days.

Wine Vinegar Curd Cheese

The method is exactly the same as for the previous recipe – you merely substitute wine vinegar for the lemon juice. Although, theoretically, ordinary malt vinegar can be used, the resulting cheese is somewhat harsh tasting, and so wine vinegar is a far better choice. Also, by purchasing a flavoured wine vinegar – garlic, tarragon, etc. – you can impart subtle flavouring into your cheese without more ado.

Panir

'The Cream of Tartar is . . . to be had at any Druggist.'
Richard Mathew in *The unlearned alchymist his antidote.* (1662)

'Cream of tartar whey, two drachms of bitartrate of potash are added to a pint of milk. The whey, diluted with water, is used as a diuretic in dropsy.'

Sydenham Society (1882)

This is a soft, slightly rubbery cheese of Indian origin. It is used in both curries and sweet recipes.

To make 7 oz.–8 oz. (198 g.–225 g.)
2 pints (1.120 lit.) milk
½ level tsp. cream of tartar
½ breakfast cup hot water

Put the milk in a pan and heat to boiling point. Dissolve the cream of tartar in the cup of hot water. Remove the milk pan from the stove and stir in the tartaric acid liquid. Continue stirring until all the milk curdles. Leave aside for 15 minutes. Pour through clean muslin, spread to line a colander with enough over the edges to be able to gather it up, balanced over a bowl. Gather the corners of the muslin together, tie securely and hang up to drain for 30 minutes. Place the curds, still wrapped in the muslin, between two plates and weight down with about 5 lb. (2.250 kg.). A couple of bags of sugar will suffice if nothing more professional is to hand. Leave for 2–2½ hours. Disrobe and cut into slices about ¼"/½ cm. thick.

Lactic Curd Cheese

'Lactic acid is contained in sour milk, and is formed from sugar by a peculiar change called the lactic fermentation.'
Sir Henry E. Roscoe (1874)

'That caused Mrs Claxton's cloudy suspicion . . . to settle into an absolute curd of sourness.'
Harper's Magazine (1883)

Bottles of lactic acid are available from any good chemist, and this cheese can be made with either whole or skimmed milk.

To make about 12 oz. (337 g.)
3 pints (1.680 lit.) milk
2 tsp. lactic acid

Pour the milk into a large pan and heat over a moderate ring until it reaches 110°F/43°C on a thermometer. Remove from stove and add the lactic acid. Stir for 30 seconds and then leave to settle for 4 hours. Drain off the majority of the whey and spoon the curds into a colander lined with a large square of scalded muslin. Tie up the muslin and hang to drain for 10 minutes – or longer if a drier cheese is desired. Turn into a tub or dish, and salt or flavour – with pepper or chives perhaps – to taste.

Buttermilk Curd Cheese

'Butter mylk . . . Nothynge nourisheth more than this mylke whan hit is newe sopped up with newe hotte breadde.'
Thomas Paynell in *Schola Salernitana* (1528)

'Whose soul is butter-milk, and song is love.'
John Wolcott (1794)

Unless you are using buttermilk that has come from unpasteurized cream, you need cultured buttermilk, as opposed to that without a culture added, to make this cheese.

To make about 8 oz. (225 **g.**)
2 pints (1.20 lit.) cultured buttermilk

Put the buttermilk into a double saucepan, or alternatively into a bowl balanced over a pan of simmering water, and heat gently until a temperature of 160°F/71°C is reached on a thermometer. The buttermilk should start to curdle at this stage. Remove from the stove, cover and leave, undisturbed, to settle for 2–2½ hours. Ladle the curds into a colander lined with a large square of scalded muslin.

Wait for a few minutes for the majority of the whey to drain away. Gather the corners of the cloth together, tie securely and hang up to drain for 1½–2 hours – the longer it is left the drier the curds will be. Scrape the curds into a bowl. You should have a pleasant tasting, albeit blandish, curd cheese with a granular texture. Salt to taste and serve with salads, jacket potatoes and so on, or mix with salad cream and use as a moreish sandwich spread.

Yoghurt Cheese

'Neither doe they (the Turks) eate much Milke, except it bee made sower, which they call Yoghurd.'
Samuel Purchas in *Pilgrimes* (1625)

'We halted to . . . refresh ourselves with a draught of yaghourt.'
Edmund O'Donavon in *The merv oasis* (1882)

This is a simple cheese to make – and a good way to 'eate Milke'. A recipe for making yoghurt at home appears later in this book.

1 pint (560 ml.) natural yoghurt, home-made or shop bought

Turn the yoghurt into a colander lined with a large square of scalded muslin. Gather up the corners and tie securely. Hang up to drain, with a bowl underneath to catch the drips, for 24–36 hours. The cheese should now be quite solid. Shape into a neat round or roll, wrap in foil and store in the refrigerator until required.

Flavourings
(1) Roll the cheese in a bowl of chopped nuts, toasted oatmeal or sesame seeds until well coated.
(2) Mix some dried fruits and/or honey into the cheese before you shape it.
(3) Decorate the cheese with chocolate flakes and glacé cherries.
(4) Work a little salt into the cheese and serve as a savoury cheese with crackers.

WHEY CHEESES

'Of all Drinks, Whey is the most relaxing.'
John Arbuthnot in *Rules of Diet* (1732)

Whilst the whey collected from cheese-making does make a pleasant enough drink, and mixes scones and cakes to an advantage, it can also be used to make yet more cheese.

Whey Curd Cheese

1 pint (560 ml.) whey
2 pints (1.120 lit.) milk
salt to taste

Put the whey in a pan – the exact quantity is really irrelevant providing that the 1:2 (whey/milk) ratio is observed – and heat slowly until the surface looks frothy and on the verge of boiling. Pour in the milk and continue to heat, stirring constantly, for 5 minutes or so. Keep the heat turned down low, as the mixture must not boil. You may have to lift the pan off the ring, at intervals, to avoid this. When it starts to curdle, remove the pan from the stove and leave aside, undisturbed, for 1½–2 hours. Spoon the curds into a muslin-lined colander, or pour through a fine sieve, and leave to drain for another 2 hours, or until the cheese is as firm as desired. Work in salt to taste and store, in a tub, in the refrigerator.

Brown Whey Cheese

Sometimes called Mysost cheese, this Norwegian cheese is not really a true cheese at all. The available whey is simply simmered in a thick-bottomed pan until it reduces to a thick treacle. It is then turned into a mould. When cold, it resembles a brown, cloudy jelly and can be sliced. I'm afraid I did not go over the moon about it – it does have a strange pungency and may be regarded as an acquired taste!

SOFT AND FANCY CHEESES.

COULOMMIER

MOULDS.

In two sections.

9d. each. **8**/- per dozen.
Boxes for packing, **9**d. dozen; **8**/- gross.

CAMBRIDGE

MOULDS.

In two sections. Wood, **2/6** each.
Boxes for packing, **11**d. dozen; **10**/- gross.

GERVAIS

MOULDS.

For 6 cheeses	**2/4**
,, 12 ,,	**3/3**

BONBON.

Same design as for Gervais cheeses, but with larger holes.

For 6 cheeses	**2/-**
,, 12 ,,	**3/6**

PAPERS for lining Moulds.

1000 .. **3/-** 10,000 .. **27/-**

PONT L'EVEQUE

MOULDS.

Oblong or Square } **6**d. each; **4/9** per dozen.
Boxes for packing, **7**d. doz.; **6**/- gross.

CAMEMBERT

MOULDS.

10d. each. **9/6** per dozen.
Boxes for packing, **9**d. doz.; **8**/- gross.
½ Camembert size, **8**d. doz.; **7**/- gross.

CREAM OR BOSTOCK

MOULDS.

With loose perforated bottom and Weighted follower.

For 2 cheeses	**3/6**
,, 4 ,,	**6/-**

PORT DU SALUT TIN MOULD, with wood follower, **2/3** each.

GORGONZOLA MOULD, 3/- each. **CAERPHILLY MOULD** and follower, **5**/- each.

OAK TUBS.

With deal lids. For the renneting of the milk.

To hold 4 galls	**9/6**
,, 6 ,,	**12/-**

STRAW MATS.

For draining all soft cheeses.

Per dozen .. **2/2**
6 dozen .. **12/-**

DRAINING BOARDS.

The cheeses are drained upon straw mats placed on these boards, so that they can be moved and turned.

Per dozen .. **6/-**

CURD LADLES.

Made of enamelled Iron. For filling Moulds.

10d. each.

DRAINING TABLE ON STAND.

With removable perforated tray.

3 ft. 3 in. long	**12/-**	6 ft. long	**19/6**
4 ft. 6 in. long	**14/6**	7 ft. 6 in. long	**37/6**

CHEESE CLOTH, 1/- per yard; or a piece of 10 yards, **9**/-

RENNET MEASURING GLASS, 1/6

THE "GLEED PRESS."

DAIRY SUPPLY CO., LTD., SOLE LICENSEES.

Awarded Special Bronze Medal by the British Dairy Farmers' Association.

An exceedingly handy and useful little Press. Specially suitable for the manufacture of all kinds of Cream and soft Cheeses, for which it is unequalled; the larger sizes are also useful for household use for tongues, brawns, &c.

No.	SIZES AND PRICES.	s.	d.
1	For ½ pint cream, round	2	6
2	,, ½ ,, square	3	0
3	,, 1 ,, round	3	6
4	,, 1 ,, oblong	4	6
5	Tongue Press, round, 6 in. by 5 in. deep	5	0
6	,, ,, 7½ in. by 6½ in. deep	6	6
7	,, ,, 12 in. by 6 in.	7	6
8	,, ,, 9 in. by 7 in.	8	0

RENNETTED CHEESES

Fresh Milk Cheeses

'A milkman in Huntingdon went to his local bookshop and stationer's, asked the young girl assistant for a round book and was told: "All our books are square."'

Peterborough in *The Daily Telegraph* (1979)

'Cows are my passion.'

Charles Dickens in *Dombey and Son* (1848)

Fresh milk cheeses are popular in many European countries – with the exception of England for some strange reason – under various different names. They are often served for starters, sprinkled with salt and pepper to add a dash of piquancy to their natural blandness. Ideally, metal or plastic cheese rings – mine are 1¾"/4½ cm. deep and 2¼"/5½ cm. across – are needed, but, if you cannot track these down, various tins or plastic tubs (but do check that the plastic is non-toxic!) can be fashioned to make suitable moulds by removing both ends.

To make 4 cheeses
2 pints (1.120 lit.) milk
½ tsp. cheese rennet
3 tsp. water, boiled and cooled
salt

Heat the milk to 95°F/35°C and remove the pan from the stove. Pour in the rennet and water mixed together, and stir for half a minute to mix well. Cover, and leave undisturbed to coagulate – about 45 minutes. Line a colander with a square of scalded muslin and stand over a bowl. Ladle the curds into the colander and leave to drain for 20 minutes. Stand the cheese rings on a plate, making sure they are level, and spoon the partially drained curds into the rings. Sprinkle with salt and leave to drain for 10 minutes.

Place another plate – preferably the same size as the one the cheeses are standing on – upside down, on top of the rings. Then, holding the plates together tightly to stop the rings from slipping, turn the cheeses upside down. This operation should be swiftly effected over the sink – unless you particularly enjoy mopping up. Lift the top plate off and sprinkle the other side of the cheeses with salt. Cover, and leave to drain for another 4 hours or so. You can hurry this process by repeating the turnabout business every 30 minutes, but, if there is no panic, just leave gravity to do its stuff. Store the cheeses in a cool place – it is best to leave them in their rings until they are served. Eat within 2 days.

Cottage Cheese

'Nothynge he hadde to conforte in age Save a melche cow, and a poore cotage.'
Alexander Barclay in *The cytezen and uplondyshman* (1514)

'On dairy farms where cheese and butter are made, pigs are useful to consume whey and skim-milk.'
J.P. Sheldon in *British Dairying* (1893)

Cottage cheese is believed to be so called – along with Cottage Pie and Cottage Loaves – because it was made by cottagers in bygone days. It was considered to be a good way of using up the skimmed milk – especially if no obliging pigs were kept with the family cow. However, although not traditional, whole milk can be used to make this cheese, and a starter culture is optional.

To make approx. 8 oz. (225 g.)
2 pints (1.120 lit.) skimmed or whole milk (skimmed milk available at Sainsbury's)
1 tbs. cultured buttermilk or natural yoghurt (optional starter)
2 tsp. junket rennet
salt to taste

Heat the milk gradually to 100°F/38°C and stir in the starter, if using, and the rennet. Cover and leave, undisturbed, for an hour to coagulate. Cut the firm curds into ½"/1 cm. cubes, and slowly re-heat to 100°F/38°C, stirring gently. Remove the pan from the stove and leave the contents to settle for 15 minutes. Line a colander with scalded muslin and stand over a bowl. Spoon in the curds and leave to drain for 10 minutes or so. Hold the colander under a running, cold water tap, and literally 'wash' the curds. This process produces the traditional lumpy texture associated with cottage cheese. Stand the colander over a bowl. Stir the lumpy curds, salt to taste, and leave to drain for a few minutes. Turn into a tub and store in the refrigerator. Chopped chives, caraway seeds or garlic salt impart interesting flavours if desired.

Cambridge (York) Cheese

'Spanish Annatto . . . is much the best for Cheese-colouring.'
Josiah Twamley in *Dairying Exemplified* (1784)

In bygone years, Cambridge cheese (which is also known as York cheese in York and some other places!) was traditionally made in a rectangular mould, about the size of a housebrick, and stood on straw mats to drain. The mats were woven from the finest harvest straw, in the winter months, by the village women. Up until the start of the Second World War (when the Ministry ordered cheese-making economies), the cheeses were made on a commercial basis by at least three Cambridgeshire makers, and the cost of a cheese was one old shilling (5p). Alas, the cheese is not made in any great quantity nowadays, and the traditional moulds and straw mats are very hard to acquire.

However, Cambridge cheese is still made by some folk in Cambridgeshire, and, with improvised equipment, anyone can produce it at home. Round or square cake tins, about 6″/15 cm. and with their bases removed, will serve as moulds, and a pad of folded muslin will suffice in lieu of a straw mat. This recipe is still used in Cambridge at the time of writing.

To make 2 cheeses
8 pints (4.480 lit.) milk
1 tsp. lactic acid
1 tsp. cheese rennet
6 tsp. boiled and cooled water
few drops of annatto colouring (optional)
salt (optional)

Heat the milk steadily in a large pan to 155°F/68°C, and then cool it as quickly as possible to 90°F/32°C. This is best effected by standing the pan in a sink of cold water and stirring until the lower temperature is reached. Add the lactic acid and stir for one minute. Leave aside for 10 minutes for the milk to ripen. Mix the rennet and water together, add to the milk and stir well. If an orange strip is desired (this is characteristic of this cheese but by no means essential – it does not affect the flavour in any way) pour about 2 pints (1.120 lit.) of the rennetted milk into a separate container and mix in a few drops of annatto. Leave to set for 30 minutes, or until the curd breaks cleanly. Meanwhile, sterilize the draining utensils, and stand the moulds (2 cake tins about 6″/15 cm. for this quantity of milk) on straw or plastic draining mats, or folded muslin, on a tray.

When set, gently pour off some of the whey from both the white and orange curds. Use a plate on top of the moulds to stop the curds going down the drain too. Next, cut 'tops' for your cheeses by pressing the moulds into the surface of the white curds – in the same way that you cut biscuits with a cutter. Carefully remove these with a cooking slice and keep on a plate to top your cheese. Ladle about two thirds of the white curds, draining off as much of the whey as possible without breaking the curds too much, into the available moulds, and then put a layer of the orange curds on top. Finally, fill the moulds with the remaining white curds and position the neatly cut tops. If the moulds are full before all this can be done, simply wait for a few minutes for some of the whey to drain off and for the curds to sink in the moulds.

It is a good idea to stand the draining tray on the draining board, by the kitchen sink, for the first hour or so's draining in case the whey overflows – as mine usually does. When the initial draining process has calmed down, pour or spoon off as much whey as possible and put the cheeses in a cool place for 2 or 3 days. By then, they should have shrunk considerably. Many authorities firmly state that Cambridge cheese is not salted at all, but this particular recipe says that they should be lightly sprinkled with salt, wrapped in greaseproof paper, and stored for another 12 hours before eating. However, the salt controversy is really a matter of personal taste.

Colwick Cheese

'Hung cheese. It is called hung when the curds are tied up in a cloth or net, to get quit of the whey . . . instead of being put under the press.'

Robert Forsyth (1806)

'Colwick Cheese – a soft English cheese once made on farms and country estates, now virtually extinct.'

Bruce H. Axler in *The Cheese Handbook* (1970)

Colwick cheese, which takes its name from the village of Colwick, near Nottingham, is rarely seen nowadays. However, it is simple enough to make, and is an unusual cheese in that it is traditionally served, with its cavity stuffed with whipped cream and fruits, as a rather extravagant dessert. The old moulds for this cheese were just like small, round cake tins, albeit with holes in both bottom and sides to encourage drainage. It is fairly easy to make an authentic tin – you need a cake tin with a diameter of about 5″/12½ cm., an electric drill and a handyman! Alternatively, a cake tin with a loose bottom removed will suffice. The rennet is mixed with rather more water than usual to produce a softer than average curd.

To make 1 cheese
4 pints (2.240 lit.) full cream milk (e.g. Jersey)
½ tsp. cheese rennet
¼ pint (140 ml.) water, boiled and cooled

Heat the milk slowly to 84°F/29°C – rather under than over this temperature, as a higher one will only result in too hard a curd. Remove from stove and stir in the rennet and water mixed together. Stir for 6 minutes, cover the pan so that the milk retains a little heat, and leave to set to a soft curd – 40 minutes. Line a colander with a large piece of scalded muslin and stand over a bowl. Ladle in the curds and leave to drain for 15 minutes. Stand a mould, as previously described, on a draining mat (or folded muslin) on a board or tray.

Take 3 corners of the muslin and tie together with the fourth. Ease into the mould. As the curd drains, the top of the cheese should curl inwards to produce the traditional, bowl-shaped Colwick cheese. Tighten the knot every 30 minutes or so, to encourage this process. The cheese can usually be disrobed after 3 or 4 hours – it should be quite firm on the outside but softish in the middle. It can be salted and served as a savoury cheese but, as previously mentioned, it is usually stuffed with cream and fruit, sprinkled with sugar (brown is best!) and served for afters.

Caerphilly Cheese

'The prohibition of Caerphilly cheese created an outcry from the miners of the West, who regarded it as an essential factor to their existence.'

Val Cheke in *The Story of Cheese-making in Britain* (1959)

As is popularly known, Caerphilly cheese takes its name from the Welsh mining town of the same name, but very little cheese is actually made in the town nowadays. It has always been a favourite with miners as it is easily digested (and so doesn't repeat on one when bending and grovelling in the coal!) and, also, the traditional 2½"/6 cm. thickness makes convenient wedges to eat down the mine.

Although Caerphilly is regarded as a hard cheese by some authorities – albeit semi-hard by others – it only needs about 4 lb./1.800 kg. to press it, and it matures in a fortnight. In comparison, Cheddar needs at least 30 lb./13.500 kg., making a cheese press absolutely necessary, and some 6 months and much patience to reach maturity. Hence, Caerphilly is the simplest of the rather harder cheeses to make, and, although a press does help, it is by no means essential.

To make one cheese weighing 2¼–2½ lb. (1.012 – 1.125 kg.)
2 gallons (8.960 lit.) milk
¼ pint (140 ml.) natural yoghurt
1½ tsp. cheese rennet
9 tsp. water, boiled and cooled
1 oz. (28 g.) salt
1 oz. (28 g.) pure lard, melted, or rice flour

Put the milk into a cheese vat, if available, or alternatively into a white plastic dairy bucket, and stand in a sink of very hot water. Stir the milk until it reaches 90° F/32°C and then stir in the natural yoghurt, mixing well. Cover the vat or bucket and drain out the water – do not leave standing in the hot water otherwise the temperature of the milk will continue to rise.

Leave the milk to sour for about half an hour, and then stir in the rennet, diluted in water. Stir deeply for one minute, and then top-stir (i.e. just the top 2") until it starts to coagulate.

Cover and leave undisturbed – and shoo all mortals who want to wash their grubby/muddy/oily/painty hands in the sink out of the kitchen – until set to a firm curd – 45–60 minutes. Cut the curd into ½"/1 cm. cubes with a sharp knife (or curd cutter if you have one of those gadgets). Fill the sink with hot water again and, stirring continuously, raise the temperature to 92°F/33°C. Technically, you should keep the curds at this temperature and stir constantly for the next 40 minutes, but if the temperature falls or rises a couple of degrees, or the phone rings, don't worry – disaster is not imminent. Anyhow, to check whether or not the curds are sufficiently 'cooked', take a small piece and press it with your fingers. If your fingerprint remains, the curd is ready, if it does not, keeping stirring at the same temperature until it does – it merely means that the acidity is only developing slowly.

When the curd is ready, leave it to 'pitch', i.e. to settle in the whey, and then pour off the whey immediately. Avoid leaving the curds in the whey for too long otherwise too much acidity will develop for this type of cheese. Pile the curds on one side of the vat, or bucket, leave 5 minutes, and pour off any more whey. Cut the curd into cubes again, leave 10 minutes, and again drain off any more whey that has accumulated. Turn the curds into a large colander lined with a large piece of muslin and stand it in the sink or on the draining board. Gather the muslin corners and transfer the curd to a scale – there should be about 3½–4 lb. (1.575 – 1.800 kg.). If your cheese still weighs considerably more, go on draining it.

Return the curds, still in the muslin, to the colander in the sink, and break into small pieces. Mix in the salt – you can use your hands, clean and scrubbed of course! Gather the muslin corners again, and fit the curds into a mould – bottomless, about 6" or 7"/15 cm. or 17½ cm. in diameter, and with holes in the sides – standing on a draining mat and board, or under a cheese press. A cake tin with its base removed and holes drilled in the sides will serve in lieu of a proper mould. Fold the top of the muslin over, making it as flat as possible, and position a follower on top, i.e. a piece, usually of wood, the same size as the mould. However, if you are using a cake tin, the removed base will suffice. Weigh down with 4 lb./1.800 kg. or adjust the press as necessary. Turn the cheese 3 times, over the next

45 minutes, at 15 minute intervals, re-applying pressure each time.

Leave under the weights for 15 hours. Disrobe and wipe with a clean cloth. Paint with melted lard, or dust with rice flour as preferred. You can bandage it if you like – just cut 2 rounds and a length of muslin to cover the cheese – but this is not really necessary for a cheese that is ready so quickly. Store in a cool, dry room for a fortnight, turning daily.

Coulommier Cheese

'The Coulommier is a small, flat, circular cheese measuring about 5½ inches in diameter by 2½ inches in thickness.
'Wrapped in butter paper and packed in a chip or card box the cheese presents a favourable appearance and will realise 8d or 9d when sold retail.'

Tisdale and Robinson (1908)

'Coulommier – whole £1.46'

Paxton & Whitfield price list (November 1979)

A popular French cheese, sometimes described as a baby Brie, Coulommier cheese can be eaten fresh or else left to ripen until a surface mould develops. As with all foreign cheeses, the authentic flavour can only be introduced with use of the correct bacteria to ripen the milk, and this is always difficult to obtain outside the area in which the cheese is commonly produced. However, a Coulommier-type cheese is easy to make, and the special, curious, two-tiered moulds are available (see Cheese-making equipment in the Glossary). The moulds measure 6″/15 cm. in height, and have 4½″/11½ cm. diameters (making cheeses slightly smaller than those described by Tisdale and Robinson), and the joint round the waist enables the top tier to be lifted off once the curds have sunk to the depths of the lower tier. Home-made moulds can be made from two tins with the same dimensions and both ends removed. These can be sellotaped together for the early draining process.

To make 2 cheeses

1 gallon (4.480 lit.) milk
1 tsp. cheese starter culture or lactic acid
1 tsp. cheese rennet
4 tsp. boiled water, cooled
salt

Pour the milk into a large pan and heat gently to 155°F/68°C. Remove the pan from the stove and plunge into a sink of cold water. Stir until the temperature lowers to 90°F/32°C, and then take out of the sink. Stir in the starter, or lactic acid, and leave 10 minutes for the milk to ripen. Dilute the rennet in the cooled, boiled water and mix into the warm milk. Top stir (i.e. stir the top 2″), for a couple of minutes, to stop the cream from rising, and then cover and leave, undisturbed, until set. It is important not to continue stirring once the coagulation has started otherwise fat will be lost, along with the whey, resulting in small, dry cheeses.

When the curd is firm, ladle slices into the moulds which have been placed on a draining mat (straw in bygone days but plastic ones are available nowadays) or else on folded muslin, on a tray. All equipment should of course be sterilized before it is used. Try to treat the curd as gently as possible – rough handling will again encourage loss of fat. Cover the moulds, and leave until the curds have subsided to the bottom section of the mould – 8 hours or overnight – and then remove the top tier. Place a fresh mat over the top of each mould (or else folded muslin on a small plate) and invert. Leave to drain again. Repeat the operation twice a day for the next two days, by which time the cheese should be quite firm. Rub the surface of the cheese with salt, and carefully wrap it in greaseproof.

Store it in the refrigerator for another 24 hours and then it is ready to eat in a fresh state. If the cheese is to be ripened, it should be kept in a dry, airy room for 2 or 3 days, ideally with a constant temperature around 65°F/18°C, until a white mould develops. Thereafter, store in a cool, dark room for a further 2–3 weeks, turning daily.

Camembert Full Fat Cheese

'Le fromage est le bisquit des ivrognes.'
(Cheese is the biscuit of drunkards.)
Grimod de la Raynière in *Almanach des Gourmands*
(1803–12)

Romanticists attribute the invention of the much esteemed French cheese, Camembert, to a certain Madame Marie Harel, who lived in Camembert in the 18th century. However, in all probability, she probably perfected a local age-old recipe, and chronicled the method. The cheese won considerably more fame when it was fitted into little, wooden boxes (designed by a Monsieur Ridel in the 1890s) and was thereafter able to travel further afield without deterioration.

To make an authentic starter for a traditional white moulded cheese such as Camembert, dissolve a small piece of shop-bought cheese, cut from just under the skin where the flavour is at its strongest, in 2–3 tbs. of boiled water, cooled to 80°F/27°C. Strain the liquid and use as required.

To make 1 cheese
4 pints (2.240 lit.) milk
2 tbs. starter (as previously described)
½ tsp. cheese rennet
2 tsp. water, boiled and cooled
salt

Heat the milk to 86°F/30° C and add the starter culture. Leave aside for 15 minutes for the milk to ripen. Re-heat to 86°F/30°C, remove from stove and stir in the rennet and water mixed together. Cover and leave undisturbed until set. A Camembert mould usually measures about 5″/12½ cm. in diameter, and 5″/12½ cm. in height. It has holes punched in the sides to facilitate drainage. However, an old coffee tin, with both ends removed and holes drilled in the sides, will suffice admirably. When the curd is firm, after an hour or so, stand the mould on a drainage mat (or folded muslin), and ladle in the curds. When the curds have sunk halfway down the mould, place a clean mat and board (or large plate) on top of the mould and invert the whole thing. Professional Camembert cheese-makers actually turn their cheeses with their hands, but novices will find it easier to upturn the whole apparatus, in the early days at any rate!

Sprinkle the surface of the cheese with a little salt, and turn thrice daily for the next 2 days. When the cheese is firm and dry, remove its mould and store in a dark, airy place, ideally with a temperature around 55°F/13°C until ripe – up to six weeks. By then it should have developed a white, mouldy coat and weigh about 10 oz./280g. Alternatively, if you don't want to wait for the cheese to ripen, it can be eaten in its fresh state.

Mozzarella

'They have a Beast very large, having a smooth thick skin without hair, called a Buffelo, which gives good milk.'
Voyage to East Indies (1665)

Mozzarella is a distinguished, spun-curd Italian cheese, which is often favoured for topping pizzas as it melts so beautifully. It is generally eaten fresh. Originally, it was always made from buffalo's milk but, nowadays, some is produced from cow's milk as there are simply not enough buffaloes around. Some Mozzarella recipes call for the use of a cheese press but I find this makes a rather hard cheese – quite unlike the real thing.

To make 1 cheese
8 pints (4.480 lit.) buffalo's or ordinary cow's milk
2–3 tbs. natural yoghurt
1 tsp. cheese rennet
6 tsp. water, boiled and cooled
salt to taste

Heat the milk gradually to 86°F/30°C and stir in the yoghurt. Cover the pan and stand in a warm place – such as an airing cupboard – overnight. Next day, check the temperature of the soured milk, and, if it has dropped more than a few degrees, re-heat to 86°F/30°C. Mix the rennet with the water and stir into the warm, soured milk. Leave on one side, undisturbed, until set – 45–60 minutes. Put the pan over a low ring. With your hands, break and gently squeeze the curds – you don't cut the curds in this recipe – until they become too hot to handle. Continue to heat gently, for another 2 or 3 minutes, stirring continuously until the curds start to 'squeak'. Tip into a large colander, lined with muslin, and leave to drain over a bowl for 5 minutes. Keep the whey. Next, turn the rubbery curds onto a board and work in the salt – one or two teaspoons to taste.

Tip onto a square of clean muslin, knot the corners tightly, and hang up to drain. Tighten the knot every 30 minutes for the next 3 hours, to coax out as much whey as possible. When the cheese is quite firm, rather resembling a piece of putty in fact, drop it, still wrapped in the muslin, into the whey, heated to 180°F/82°C. Leave the cheese in the whey until it is cold, and then hang it up to drain for another 12 hours. Disrobe and use as required.

1 The Chamois Goat

2 Heath Ram of the Improved Breed

3 The Many-Horned Sheep

4 The Wallachian Sheep

5

6 The Tartarian Sheep

7

8

GOAT'S MILK CHEESES

'The woman grated over it a goat's milk cheese.'
Buckley (1848)

Goat's milk can be used to make any of the cheeses in this book, but the rennet should be added at a slightly lower temperature than when cow's milk is used. An increasing number of people are becoming goat-keepers – goats take up less room than cows, that's for sure – and the surplus milk is easily turned into cheeses. Mrs S. Humber of Wellington Farm, Cheddar Gorge in Somerset, makes and sells fresh goat's cheeses and yoghurt (and goat's milk too – frozen to withstand hot car journeys!). As the fresh white cheeses tend to be a bit bland, she specializes in adding various flavourings – garlic, mixed herbs, poppy seeds, paprika, and even whisky marmalade! She makes about twenty different cheeses in all. The following recipe, a traditional one, was kindly given to me by Mrs Humber.

Fresh Goat's Milk Cheese

To make 2 small cheeses
4 pints (2.240 lit.) fresh goat's milk
½ tsp. cheese rennet
2 tbs. water, boiled and cooled
salt
flavouring – chives, garlic, walnuts or whatever

Heat the milk slowly to 90°F/32°C and leave, undisturbed, for 2 hours, to ripen. Mix the rennet and water. Stir the milk clockwise and pour in the rennet anti-clockwise – this mixes in the rennet quickly without too much stirring. Leave, undisturbed, for another 2 hours, or until it has set to a firm curd. Line a colander with a square of boiled muslin, with enough over the edges to gather up, and stand over a bowl. Cut the curd and ladle into the muslin. Leave to drain for 1 hour, scraping the dried curds round the edge towards the centre, from time to time, to hasten the drainage. Tie up the corners of the cloth and hang to drip overnight.

Next day, turn into a bowl and mix in salt to taste. The cheese can be eaten plain, but one of Mrs Humber's flavourings turns the cheese into a gourmet's speciality. Cheese with chopped walnuts mixed into the curd is one of her best sellers. When the chosen flavouring has been worked into the drained curds, simply shape the curds into small rounds. The cheeses are quite happy in the freezer and so a large batch, with assorted flavourings, can be made at one time if the supply of goat's milk is plentiful.

Feta Cheese

The Greeks eat more cheese per head than any other country – any holidaymaker, having ploughed through endless Greek salads with the inevitable *feta* will verify that! Traditionally, *feta* cheese is made with ewe's milk, but much *feta* produced now (even in Greece!) is made from bleached cow's milk, sometimes with the addition of some ewe's milk and/or goat's milk. *Feta* should be very white, moist and crumbly, and have a salty-sour taste. Anyhow, goat's milk, which is more readily available than ewe's milk, makes quite a good imitation *feta*. Simply follow the previous recipe for Fresh Goat's Milk Cheese but save the whey. Store this in a sterilized bottle in the fridge until required. After the curds have been drained overnight, place them (still in the muslin) between two plates and weight down so as to extract the last few drops of whey. Leave for another 6–12 hours until quite hard. Disrobe the flattened curd, sprinkle with salt and put in a container. Cover with a mixture – 50/50 – of the saved whey and brine. Store in a cool place for 3–4 days to pickle itself – *feta* is often referred to as a 'pickled cheese'.

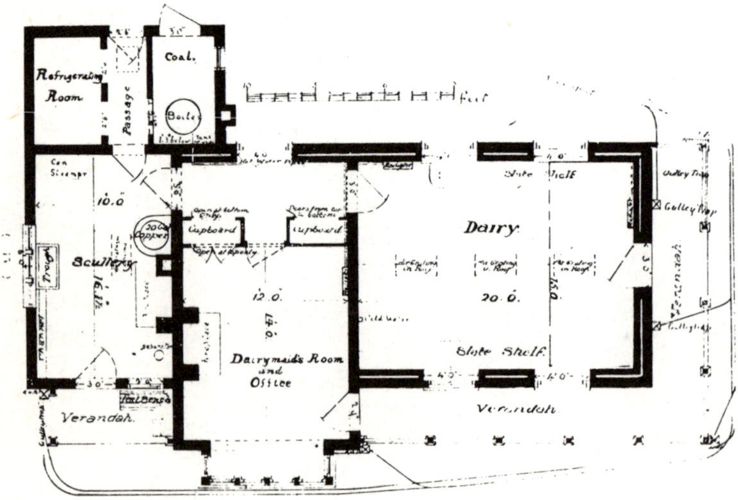

PLAN OF PRIVATE DAIRY BELONGING TO L. DICKSON PAGE, ESQ.

CREAM CHEESES

Single Cream Cheese

'An English gentleman may believe that the world was made by chance, or the moon made of cream-cheese, if he pleases.'
Abraham Tucker in *The light of nature pursued* (1768–74)

½ pint (280 ml.) single cream
2 tbs. natural yoghurt
1 tsp. junket rennet
salt

Heat the cream gently to 100°F/38°C. Stir in the yoghurt and keep the pan over the heat until the temperature of the mixture reaches 100°F/38°C again. Transfer to either an insulated food flask or wide necked vacuum flask, and leave for 2 hours for the cream to thicken and sour. Incidentally, ready soured cream (available from a few shops) can be used for this recipe, in which case this prelimary operation is not necessary.

Pour the soured cream into a small bowl and stand in a large pan of simmering water. Heat gently until 100°F/38°C is reached – this should only take a few seconds, as the idea of putting the cream into an insulated container is to maintain its temperature, thus encouraging the souring process – and then mix in the rennet. Remove the pan from the heat and cover immediately, leaving the bowl in the hot water, undisturbed, for 2 hours or until set. Turn into a muslin-lined colander, tie up the corners of the cloth and hang to drain for 8–12 hours. Scrape the cheese into a bowl, salt to taste, pat into a round or sausage shape and wrap in greaseproof paper. Store in the fridge and eat within 3 days.

N.B. Double cream can also be used for this recipe if a slightly richer cream cheese is desired.

An Excellent Cream Cheese

19th century receipt

This recipe calls for raw (i.e. unpasteurized) cream, and, in view of the quantity needed, it is really only practical for cow owners to make.

'Put a quart [1.120 lit.] of good cream aside to become sour and very thick, then lay a piece of thin calico inside a small hair sieve, taking care that the calico comes quite to the top, and rather above it, in order that you may be able to pull out the cheese without any difficulty; let the sieve stand upon a dish; pour the cream into the sieve and leave it to drain. Pour away the whey from the dish every morning. In about three days the cheese will be a proper consistency and fit to eat – as thick as butter, and very delicious. If the cream will not all go into the sieve at once, pour it in during the day, as the rest sinks from the whey leaving it.

'At Dieppe little baskets are sold (heart-shape) for making cheeses, and answer the purpose exceedingly well, being very open, so that the whey drains through the calico into the dish.'

To Make Cream Cheese with Old Cheshire

'A Cheshire Cheese . . . at 10d p. lb.'
R. Langford in *An introduction to trade and business* (1809)

'Take a pound and half of old Cheshire Cheese, shave it all very thin, then put it in a Mortar, and add to it a quarter of an ounce of Mace beaten fine and sifted, half a pound of fresh Butter, and a glass of Sack; mix and beat all these together till they are perfectly incorporated; then put it in a Pot, what thickness you please, and cut it out in Slices for Cream Cheese, and serve it with the Desert.'

The above recipe, which is actually quite delectable, comes from *The Complete Housewife,* published in 1728. An easier to follow half yield version reads –

To make approx. 1 lb.
12 oz. (337 g.) Cheshire cheese, grated
good pinch of mace
4 oz. (112 g.) butter, softened
½ glass sherry

Blend all together until well mixed and then smooth into a pot or foil container. Chill, invert onto a plate, and slice to serve – minus the Sahara I rather think!

Paska

This old Russian recipe is often made in an earthenware flower pot – a new, sterilized one, of course, not one that has borne last year's geraniums.

8 oz. (225 g.) cream cheese
5 fl.oz. (one small tub) natural yoghurt
2 oz. (56 g.) unsalted butter
1 tbs. each of raisins, candied peel, sultanas, ground mixed nuts
8 glacé cherries, halved

Blend all the ingredients together with a fork. Line a clean flower pot with a large piece of sterilized muslin. Pack the cream cheese mixture into the pot (one with a 4″ or 5″ diameter is suitable) and fold the muslin neatly over the top. Stand in a dish – to catch any small quantity of whey that may seep out – and weight down. Leave for 12–24 hours in a cool place, and then invert onto a serving dish. Small slices of the *paska* can be served as a dessert cake – it is very rich!

DAIRY SHOP UTENSILS.

COUNTER PANS.

THE "HOOPED" PAN.

(Round).

Introduced by the Dairy Supply Co., Ltd.

VERY STRIKING AND BOLD.

Have sold in large numbers.

In three styles—Maroon and Gold, Blue and Gold, or Green and Gold, with "New Milk" in gold letters.

	£	s.	d.
Capacity 12 quarts ..	**1**	**10**	**0**
" 18 " ..	**2**	**10**	**0**

THE "MAYFAIR" PAN.

(Oval).

Registered and Sold only by the Dairy Supply Company, Limited.

NOVEL AND VERY HANDSOME DESIGN.

The best class pan that is made. In different colours—Yellow, Pink, Maroon, Light Green, Dark Green, and Salmon, freely decorated in Gold, "New Milk" in gold letters, and festoons of wild flowers in natural colours.

	£	s.	d.
Capacity—18 quarts ..	**2**	**15**	**0**

THE "FLUTED" PAN.

(Round).

Introduced by the Dairy Supply Co., Ltd.

EFFECTIVE AND NEW PATTERN.

In three styles—Maroon and Gold, Blue and Gold, or Green and Gold, with "New Milk" in gold letters.

	£	s.	d.
Capacity—18 quarts ..	**2**	**10**	**0**

THE "ALBION" PAN.

(Round).

A cheap and attractive Pan.

In Pure White with "New Milk" in plain bold black letters.

	s.	d.
Capacity—12 quarts.. ..	**12**	**6**
" 18 "	**18**	**0**

THE "CREAM" PAN.

(Round).

A small size suitable for cream.

Capacity—About 4 quarts.. .. **11/-**

THE "APPLE BLOSSOM" PAN.

(Round).

White ground decorated with flowers, in colours and gold. "New Milk" in gold letters. A pretty pan at a low price.

	s.	d.
Capacity—12 quarts.. ..	**17**	**0**
" 18 "	**23**	**0**

THE "PUNCH" BOWL.

(Round).

Capacity 12 quarts **18/-**

THE "PLAIN" PAN.

(Round).

Plain white earthenware with "New Milk" in black letters.

	s.	d.
Capacity—4 quarts	**2**	**10**
" 6 "	**3**	**8**
" 10 "	**5**	**6**
" 14 "	**7**	**0**
" 18 "	**8**	**6**
" 20 "	**11**	**6**
" 24 "	**13**	**0**

THE "GLOBE" PAN.

(Round).

With coloured flowers and Sprays, and "New Milk" in black letters. Gold band round top edge.

	s.	d.
Capacity—15 quarts.. ..	**15**	**0**

BLUE & WHITE JUNKET BOWLS.

	s.	d.
9 inches diameter ..	**3**	**6**
10 " " ..	**4**	**0**
12 " " ..	**5**	**6**

PLEASE NOTE.—All gilt on these Pans is BEST GOLD. Pans decorated with LIQUID GOLD are cheaper, but the gold soon washes off.

MISCELLANEOUS
OLD CHEESE RECEIPTS

The following recipes are included as much for their historical appeal as for anything else. Even so, they are workable – although some need raw cream or milk as they date from pre-pasteurization days! Novice cheese-makers are advised to follow the more contemporary recipes first, to acquaint themselves with the science of making cheeses, before embarking on these older recipes.

Milk Cheese

19th century receipt

Five quarts of new milk
Two tablespoonfuls of rennet water (rennet and water mixture)

'Put five quarts of warm milk into a bowl with two large spoonfuls of rennet water. When the curd is formed, break it gently with the hand, drawing it to the side of the basin or bowl. Let it stand for two hours; spread a cheesecloth over a sieve or round basket, put in the curd, let it drain until all the whey is off, and then salt it to your taste. Lay a cloth in a cheese-hoop, put in the curd, and lay a cloth over it. Put a wooden cover the size of the inside of the hoop over, place a two pound weight upon it, and let it remain for twelve hours; then take it out, put it in a frame, or tie a cloth tightly round it, and turn it from one side to the other every day until dry; then rub the outside with a little butter, and sprinkle some pepper over to keep the flies from it. Put it to ripen between two pewter plates. If the weather is warm it will be ready in three weeks; if cold, it will require a longer time.'

To Make a Fresh Cheese
1728

'Take a quart of Cream, and set it over the Fire till it is ready to bowl; then beat nine Eggs, yolks and whites very well; when you are beating them put to them as much Salt as will lie on a small Knife's point; put them to the Cream and some Nutmeg quartered, and tyed up in a Rag; so let them boil till the Whey is clear; then take it off the Fire, and put it in a Pan, and gather it as you do a Cheese; then put it in a Cloth, and drain it between two; then put it in a Stone Mortar and grind it, and season it with a little Sack and Orange-flower Water and Sugar, and then put it in a little earthen Colander, and let it stand two hours to drain out the Whey; then put it in the middle of a China Dish, and pour thick Cream about it; so serve it to the Table.'

Napkin Cheese

late 19th century receipt

'Put one pint of thick cream and a teaspoonful of salt into a cloth, which should be placed in a sieve the size of a teasaucer. Let it stand for twenty-four hours; then turn it. The day following it will be ready to serve.'

Artificial Cheese

c. 1893

One gallon of new milk
Two quarts of cream
Six or eight eggs
Six or seven tablespoons of wine vinegar
A little salt

'Boil one gallon of milk with two quarts of cream; add six or eight eggs well beaten, and six or seven large spoonfuls of wine vinegar. Let it simmer until it comes to a tender curd, then tie it in a cheese-cloth, and hang it to drain for several hours; after which, open the cloth, work some salt to the cheese, then lay a cloth in a colander or cheese-hoop, put the curd in, fold the cloth over, and lay a heavy weight upon it for one hour, or longer; then turn it on a dish and serve.'

To Make a Brick-Bat Cheese. It must be made in September

H. Glasse's receipt (1796)

'Take two gallons of new milk, and a quart of good cream, heat the cream, put in two spoonfuls of rennet, and when it is come, break it a little, then put it into a wooden mould, in the shape of a brick. It must be half a year old before you eat it: you must press it a little, and so dry it.'

To Make Sage Cheese

'Bruise the tops of some young red sage in a mortar with some leaves of spinach, and squeeze the juice; mix it with the rennet in the milk, more or less according as you like the colour and taste. When the curd has come, break it gently, and put it in with the skimmer till it is pressed two inches above the vat. Press it eight or ten hours, salt it, and turn it every day.'

Snow Cheese
19th century

1 pint (560 ml.) thick cream
¼ lb. (112 g.) double refined loaf sugar
juice of 2 lemons
peel of 3 lemons, grated

'Mix with a pint of thick cream a quarter of a pound of double-refined loaf sugar, the juice of two lemons, the peel of three grated. Whisk the whole up until quite thick, put it into a lawn sieve just large enough to hold the quantity, and let it stand twenty-four hours before you turn it into a dish for the table.'

Cottenham Cheese

'In preparing the rennet for the purpose of making cheese, which in several parts of the county, particularly in the parishes of Cottenham, Waterbeach, and Denny Abbey, is brought to great perfection, nothing more is necessary than salting down the bags, in which state they remain for twelve months. About six of these bags will make two gallons of brine, strong enough to suspend a new laid egg, which being put into a jar is fit for use in about a month, when a gill of it to every four gallons of new milk, or warm as from the cow, is sufficient; the milk should all be of the same age, or meal, and much depends upon breaking the curds, with the hands, for unless that is done very completely the whey cannot be expressed, any of which remaining in the cheese, communicates a harsh fiery taste, produces blue mould, and leaves the cheese full of holes or cells, like a honey-comb. In short the dairy maid's attention should never be called off or diverted from the very essential process of breaking the curd.

'The superiority of Cottenham cheese, so famous through England, is not be be ascribed to any particular mode in the management of the dairies, but solely to the nature of the herbage on the commons.'

G.A. Cooke in *Topographical and statistical description of the county of Cambridge* (1807)

The humorous side of Farm Life No 3

FARM SNOBBERY.

Mrs. Mutt-Onn. "Did you ever see such a thing in all your life as the way these cows fancy themselves lately?"
Mrs. Porker. "Hush, haven't you heard? Its because we've had a Hinman Milking Plant installed on the farm."

How to Save Labour.

Co-op. Farm, Yaxley,
Peterboro'.

GENTLEMEN, May, 1918.

The Hinman Milker is running satisfacforily and I am satisfied with it in every way. Cows milked during the second season with the machine are satisfactory; I do not see any difference with them.

It is a great saving of labour, especially in hay and harvest time; *when we are busy I can send a Man and Boy to do the work where I should have to send about half a dozen.*

In my opinion it is quite equal to hand milking, and cows properly handled do not deteriorate in any way by being milked with the Hinman Machine.

(Signed) **F. Thomason,**
Manager.

The HINMAN Milker – a One-Man Job

No two men milk alike. The Hinman machine is always the same. With it you do not need to keep your best men in the dairy to do the milking. Even a boy can milk from 18 to 25 cows an hour. The other men can be in the fields raising bigger crops.
The Hinman is simple to work, easy to clean. Low in first cost, low in upkeep. There is no complicated installation, no vacuum tank, no air pipe lines, no small rubber hose. Each unit acts separately. It is the milker that does not injure the cow.

Send for Free Catalogue.

You should read our new large Catalogue. It shows you how to increase your herds and your profits and why the Hinman pays for itself in a few months. Write to-day.

Associated Manufacturers' Co., 72-80, Mansell Street, London, E. 1.

CHEESCAKES

The name cheesecake has been applied to numerous concoctions all over the world, for centuries – some of which do not contain so much as an ounce of cheese. However, there follows a cross-section of the most delectable that do!

Cheesecake with Sultanas

'Some make with butter, cheese and yolkes of egges . . . cheese cakes, talmouses and little Lenten loaves.'

Richard Surflet (1600)

The pastry

4 oz. (112 g.) plain brown flour
4 oz. (112 g.) plain white flour
4 oz. (112 g.) butter
1 level tbs. sugar
1 large egg, beaten
approx 1 tbs. cold water

The filling

12 oz. (337 g.) curd cheese
2 oz. (56 g.) butter, softened
3 oz. (84 g.) sugar
3 eggs, separated
2–3 tbs. sultanas
grated rind of 1 lemon or few drops of lemon essence
1 level tbs. cornflour

First make the pastry. Sieve the flours together and rub in the butter to make a breadcrumb-like mixture. Stir in the sugar, the beaten egg and sufficient cold water to mix to a dough. Leave to rest for 15 minutes. Grease a flan tin – approx 8″/20 cm. in diameter and preferably with a removable base. Roll the pastry out to a rough round, slightly larger than the tin, and fit into the tin. Trim off the rough edges and prick the base with a fork.

Mash the cheese, butter, sugar and egg yolks together until well blended. Mix in the sultanas, grated rind of lemon (or essence) and cornflour. Beat the whites until stiff and fold into the mixture. Smooth into the pastry shell and bake at 350°F or Gas mark 4 for 50–60 minutes. Cut when cold.

Creamy Yoghurt Cheesecake

'Effeminate he sat, and quiet; Strange product of a cheese-cake diet.'

Matthew Prior in *Alma* (1718)

This makes a small cheesecake – ideal if you (or your figure) cannot face cheesecake for a week. The flavours of both the jelly and jam can be changed to suit personal whim.

6 digestive biscuits, crushed
1 level tsp. nutmeg
2 oz. (56 g.) butter
½ packet lemon jelly
1 tbs. water
4 oz. (112 g.) single cream cheese
4 tbs. natural yoghurt
3–4 tbs. blackberry or blackcurrant jam

Put the biscuit crumbs, nutmeg and butter into a pan over a lowish heat. Mix around until the butter melts and soaks up the crumbs. Press the mixture into the base of a 6″/15 cm. round cake tin – one with a removable base if available. Melt the jelly in the water over a low heat, and stir into the cream cheese and yoghurt, previously blended. Mix well – an electric blender may be used if desired. Leave for 20 minutes, or until nearly set, and then spoon on top of the crumb base. Chill in the refrigerator for a couple of hours. Melt the jam over a low heat, simmer for a minute to thicken, and then remove from the stove. Stir for another minute to prevent a skin from forming as it cools, and then pour over the set cake. Chill again before serving.

Swaledale Cheesecake

'. . . and whilst the beef was roasting the cheese-cakes pastry was made. They did not weigh ingredients: they rubbed butter (no margarine in those days) into the flour until it would "nip", then to crown all, they wetted it with the dripping from the roast beef, and not content with that, they ate the cheese cakes to the beef instead of bread. I wonder what they felt like after a meal like that? The sinner section doped the cheese cakes in rum as well.'

Edith Blenkiron, writing about Whitsun festivities in the Dales in bygone days, quoted by Peggy Hutchinson in *Old English Cookery* (1973)

These cheesecakes are specialities of the Dales.

To make 2 cakes

12 oz. (337 g.) shortcrust pastry (made with butter!)
1 lb. (450 g.) curd cheese, unsalted
2 eggs, beaten
2 tbs. double cream
4 oz. (112 g.) butter, softened
4 oz. (112 g.) sugar
grated rind of 1 lemon
1 level tsp. nutmeg
3 tbs. currants
milk for glaze

Roll out the pastry thinly and line two sandwich tins – approx. 7"/17½ cm. in diameter. Save all the trimmings to make lattice-work tops. Mash the curd cheese with the beaten eggs, cream and butter to make a smooth mixture, and then work in the sugar, lemon rind, nutmeg and currants. Mix well. Divide the mixture between the 2 pastry shells, and smooth over with the back of a spoon. Roll out the pastry trimmings and cut thin strips. Arrange over the cakes to make a lattice work design. Stick in place with milk, as necessary, and brush with milk to encourage a golden colour. Bake at 375°F or Gas mark 5 for 30–35 minutes.

Coffee and Walnut Cheesecake

'A sort of cheese-cake, made of cheese, eggs and butter.'
Alexis Soyer in *The Pantropheon* (1853)

To make 1 cake
8 digestive biscuits
1 oz. (28 g.) walnuts, broken
2 oz. (56 g.) butter, melted
¼ pint (140 ml.) milk
2 eggs, separated
2 oz. (56 g.) caster sugar
2 tsp. instant coffee powder
1 sachet gelatine
8 oz. (225 g.) curd cheese
10 walnut halves for decoration

Crush the digestive biscuits. The easiest way to do this is to lay them flat in a plastic bag and then roll them firmly with a rolling pin. Mix with the broken walnut pieces and melted butter, and press into a lightly greased flan tin – 8″/20 cm. Chill in the refrigerator while you prepare the filling.

Put the milk, egg yolks, sugar and coffee powder into a double saucepan – or bowl balanced over a pan of simmering water – and stir until well blended. Sprinkle over the gelatine, and continue stirring until completely dissolved. Remove from heat and leave to cool but do not let it set. Fork the curd cheese and mix into the cooled coffee mixture. Transfer, ideally, to a blender and whisk away until very smooth. Beat the egg whites until stiff and fold into the coffee cheese mixture. Pour over the chilled biscuit base, and decorate with walnut halves. Chill for at least four hours, or overnight, before serving.

To Make Cheesecakes without Rennet 1728

'Take a quart of thick Cream, and set it over a clear Fire with some quartered Nutmeg in it: just as it boils up, put in twelve Eggs well beaten, and a quarter of a pound of fresh Butter; stir it a little while on the Fire, till it begins to curdle; then take it off, and gather the Curd as for Cheese; put it in a clean Cloth, tye it together, and hang it up that the Whey may run from it; when 'tis pretty dry, put it in a Stone Mortar, with a pound of Butter, a quarter of a pint of thick Cream, some Sack or Orange flower-water, and half a pound of fine Sugar; then beat and grind all these very well together for an hour or more till 'tis very fine, then pass it through a hair Sieve, and fill your Pattipans but half full. You may put Currants in half the quantity, if you please: A little more than a quarter of an hour will bake them. Take the Nutmegs out of the Cream when 'tis boiled.'

CREAM

'A new class finds itself at the top, as certainly as cream rises in a bowl of milk.'

Ralph W. Emerson in *Essays* (1841–44)

Unlike cheese or butter which need some assistance to take shape, cream does not have to be made; it appears as a matter of course. It is, in fact, the butyraceous or fatty part of milk. This fat content, of which cream is mainly composed, is somewhat lighter than the liquid part of milk, and so the fat globules rise automatically when a pan of milk is left to 'cream'. Twenty-four hours is usually reckoned to be a period long enough for this process to take place – providing, of course, that the pan is not knocked or disturbed in any way. The surface cream is then simply skimmed off with the help of a skimmer – a scallop shell serves the purpose admirably as the grooves let the milk run off freely. With this old fashioned method of skimming milk, a small portion of the cream always gets left behind, and so most commercial dairies use a mechanical separator which spins off the cream with exacting efficiency. Thus shop-bought cream is always of one of the classified types – single, double or whipping consistency. Clotted cream is not so prolific but is certainly the richest available.

Fig. 19.
g. 18.
10.

Clotted Cream for Impatient People

'She would . . . give hem Curds and clouted Creame.'
Edmund Spenser in *The Shepheardes* (1579)

Heat the cream – pasteurized or raw – in a bowl over a pan of simmering water until it reaches 170°F/76°C. Stir it once or twice to distribute the heat, but, thereafter, do not stir again. Continue to raise the temperature of the cream to about 180°F/82°C and maintain this temperature – give or take a few degrees either way but definitely not above 190°F/87°C – for one hour. Carefully lift the bowl off the pan – the cream at this stage looks wrinkled and none too inviting – and stand it in a larger bowl (which can be a plastic washing-up one) full of cold water and ice cubes. The idea is to cool the cream as rapidly as possible. Once cool, leave the bowl in a cool place where it will not get knocked for 8 hours or overnight. Next day, lift off the thick, rich clot or 'cloutie' of cream from the skim milk and store in a lidded pot or jar, in the refrigerator, until required.

To Scald Cream, as in the West of England
c. 1893

'Smearing both with Devonshire cream and with honey.'
Boy's Own Paper (August 10th, 1889)

This is a more traditional recipe for clotted cream, and calls for milk with a high fat content and well defined creamline, e.g. Jersey milk or South Devon milk, for best results.

'Strain the milk into large shallow pans about three or four inches deep, and let it stand twenty-four hours; then place the pan very carefully upon a hot plate, or slow fire, to heat gently, taking care it does not boil, or there will be a skin instead of a cream upon the milk. As soon as the cream forms a ring round the pan, and the undulations on the surface look thick, it is done; then remove it from the fire into the dairy, and let it remain for twenty-four hours, or if in cold weather, thirty-six; then skim it for use. The butter usually made in Devonshire of cream thus prepared is very firm and good.'

Cambridge or Burnt Cream

This very rich dessert originates from Trinity College, Cambridge, where it was much favoured by the scholars in the late 19th century.

6 egg yolks
8 oz. (225 g.) caster sugar
1 pint (560 ml.) single cream
ice cubes

Fork the egg yolks with a tablespoon of the sugar. Pour the cream into a pan, bring to the boil, and pour over the egg yolks. Transfer to a double saucepan, or else balance the bowl over a pan of simmering water. Heat very gently (do not let it boil or else you will have Curdled Cream!) until it thickens sufficiently to coat the back of a spoon. Transfer to an oven dish and bake at 300°F or Gas mark 2 until set. Leave to cool. Sprinkle with the rest of the sugar, to form a thick crust, and stand the dish in a large tin with plenty of ice cubes. The ice stops the heat from curdling the set cream. Place under a very hot grill until the sugar caramelizes. Serve cold.

Coffee Cream

'Coffee (which makes the politician wise,
And see through all things with his half-shut eyes).'
Pope in *Rape of the Lock* (1712–14)

This is nearly as simple as powdered instant dessert but is far more delectable.

1½ tsp. powdered gelatine
4–5 tbs. very strong coffee (if you want to be wise!)
3 oz. (84 g.) sugar
½ pint (280 ml.) thick whipping cream

Put the gelatine, hot coffee and sugar into a liquidizer and blend until the gelatine and sugar have completely dissolved. Leave to cool, but not to set, while you whip the cream. Fold the liquid gelatine into the whipped cream, pour into dishes or glasses and leave to set.

ICE-CREAM

'We dare not trust our wit for making our house pleasant to our friend, and so we buy ice-creams.'

Emerson (1841)

Ice-cream was probably first made by the Chinese some 2,000 years ago, but one of England's first encounters with it could have been at Henry V's Coronation when a certain *crême frez* was served. Later tradition maintains that Charles I paid his French chef the sum of £20 a year to keep his ice-cream recipe a royal secret.

At the beginning of this century, the Italians were the chief makers and sellers of ice-cream in England. Their handcarts plied for trade throughout the streets of London, and the following jingle was constantly heard –

Ice-Cream

Hokey-Pokey
Penny a lump,
That's the stuff
To make you jump!

Indeed, 'Hokey-Pokey' is claimed to be a derivative of the Italian *Ecco un poco*, meaning 'Here is a little'. Many Italian ices are still to be found all over England, with the old Italian names – Rossi, Tomassi, etc. – still doing brisk business. However, American style ice-cream parlours, with their umpteen flavours, are blossoming everywhere. Thus, there is no shortage of commercially produced ice-cream for sale.

Investment in an ice-cream maker is necessary if you hope to produce a commercial type of ice-cream. These machines are filled with the ice-cream mixture and then put in the freezer. Small paddles rotate merrily, as the mixture freezes, and this movement incorporates air into the mixture and stops the formation of hard ice particles. However, delectable ice-creams can be made without the expense of such gadgetry – the inclusion of gelatine in the recipes helps to keep them soft. There are two basic recipes for home-made ice-cream; one is quite simply frozen, flavoured cream, whereas the other is a mixture of custard and cream. These simple rules apply to all the ice-cream recipes that follow –

1. Always use fresh ingredients and scrupulously clean utensils.
2. Mix the ingredients according to the recipe.
3. After the initial mixing, pour the mixture into a chilled freezer tray. Leave to semi-freeze for 30–45 minutes – until the edges are frozen, but the centre is still mushy.
4. Turn into a bowl and stir until smooth. This process incorporates air into the mixture and helps to break down the ice particles. The operation may be repeated after another hour if time and patience permit.
5. Return the mixture to the freezer either in the same freezer tray – washed out and dried – or else in a plastic bowl or tub with a lid. The latter facilitates storage.
6. Prior to serving the ice-cream, remove it from the freezer and leave it in the fridge to soften slightly. Half an hour is usually sufficient but experience will prove the best judge.

Pineapple Ice-Cream

'Toby, take that load of pine apple ice into the ball-room, and present an ice to each lady.'
T. & J. M. Morton *All That Glitters* (1850)

Although pineapple ice-cream sounds quite exotic, this very simple version can be conjured up in no time at all – from store-cupboard ingredients!

½ pint (280 ml.) milk, chilled
2 sachets Dream Topping
small tin of crushed pineapple, drained

Mix up the Dream Topping as indicated on the packet and smooth into a freezer tray. Semi-freeze for 30 minutes. Turn into a bowl and stir until smooth again. Mix in the crushed pineapple and turn into a tub. Freeze until firm.

Plain White Ice-Cream – Italian Style

'These Italian ice-cream men, with their heavy barrows.'
A. T. Pask (1889)

½ pint (280 ml.) milk
1 tbs. cornflour (white)
4 tbs. granulated sugar
¼ pint (140 ml.) whipping cream
1 egg white

Blend the cornflour with 2 tbs. of the milk. Heat the rest of the milk in a pan, with the sugar, over a gentle heat, until the sugar dissolves completely. Pour the hot milk over the cornflour paste, stir, and return to pan. Continue to heat until the custard thickens and coats the back of a spoon. Remove from heat and stir until cool. Pour into a chilled freezer tray and freeze until semi-frozen – 45 minutes approx. Whip the cream and egg white separately until stiff. Mash the semi-frozen custard and blend into the whipped cream, and then the egg white. Return to the freezer tray – rinsed out then dried – and freeze again for 45 minutes. Turn into a bowl and stir again to break up the ice pieces. Turn into a plastic box or tub (preferably with a lid) and freeze until firm. This takes 2–4 hours depending on the type of freezer. Remember to transfer to the fridge, to soften a little, a while before serving.

Vanilla Ice-Cream Made with Custard

1 egg
4 oz. (112 g.) vanilla sugar
½ pint (280 ml.) milk
¼ pint (140 ml.) double cream
1 egg white

Beat the whole egg with the vanilla sugar (vanilla essence and ordinary sugar can be used but vanilla sugar is infinitely better) in a bowl. Boil the milk and pour over the beaten egg mixture. Stir well and balance the bowl over a pan of simmering water. Cook over a gentle heat until the mixture thickens and coats the back of a spoon. Allow to cool and then pour into a freezer tray. Remove from the freezer when semi-frozen, turn into a bowl and stir until smooth. Whip the double cream and egg white until stiff and fold into the custard. Transfer to a lidded tub and freeze until firm.

Lemon Ice-Cream

4 oz. (112 g.) cream cheese or lemon curd cheese
grated rind and juice of 1 lemon
3 tbs. sifted icing sugar
few drops of lemon colouring (optional)
$\frac{1}{4}$ pint (140 ml.) double cream
1 egg white

Mash the cheese with the lemon rind and juice, icing sugar and colouring if using. Whip the double cream and egg white until stiff and fold into the lemon-cheese mixture. Turn into a freezer tray and freeze until the edges are solid. Turn into a bowl, stir until smooth and transfer to a container. Freeze until firm.

Black Cherry Yoghurt Ice-Cream

'The company are entertained with ice in several forms . . .'
Lady M.W. Montagu (October 1st, 1716)

Yoghurt, of course, can be frozen on its own, but it does also make a very good ice-cream when mixed with cream. The black cherry flavouring makes a slightly sharp, albeit very refreshing, ice-cream. However, any flavour can be used – or even natural with a tablespoon or so of honey for sweetening. Ice-cream without any sugar at all goes incredibly hard!

¼ pint (140 ml.) double cream
1 egg white
¼ pint (140 ml.) black cherry yoghurt

Whip the cream and egg white until stiff and then fold in the yoghurt. Freeze in a freezer tray until hard around the edges and then turn into a bowl. Stir until smooth. Transfer to a plastic tub with a lid and freeze until firm.

Quick-Setting Jelly Ice-Cream

1 envelope quick-setting jelly (any flavour as desired)
3–4 tbs. sugar
$\frac{1}{3}$ pint (186 ml.) cold water
4 oz. (112 g.) cream cheese
$\frac{1}{4}$ pint (140 ml.) double cream

Dissolve the jelly powder and sugar in cold water, in a pan over a low heat. Bring to the boil and boil for a few minutes until the mixture thickens and clears. Remove from heat and stir until cool but not set. Soften the cream cheese and blend with the jelly. This can be done in an electric blender if available. Whip the cream into peaks and fold in the creamed mixture. Turn into a chilled freezer tray and freeze until semi-frozen. Turn into a bowl and stir until smooth. Transfer to a plastic container and freeze until firm – one hour plus, according to freezer.

Old-Fashioned Strawberry Ice-Cream

'Curly locks, curly locks,
Wilt thou be mine?
Thou shalt not wash dishes, nor yet feed the swine,
But sit on a cushion and sew a fine seam,
And feed upon strawberries, sugar and cream.'
Nursery Rhyme (Traditional)

This must be one of the simplest ice-creams in the world.

½ pint (280 ml.) double cream
1 egg white (optional)
2 tbs. thick strawberry jam – preferably home-made

Whip the cream with the egg white (if using). Stir in the strawberry jam – don't worry about getting it too evenly distributed. Put in a freezer tray and freeze until the edges are hard but the centre still runny. Turn into a bowl and stir until smooth. Transfer to a plastic container and freeze until firm.

Brown Bread Ice-Creams

Although a seemingly strange ingredient for ice-cream, brown bread gives it an interesting texture and has, in fact, been used in ices for several hundred years. Frederick Nutt in his *The Complete Confectioner* (1789), gave a recipe calling for a pint of double cream and two handfuls of breadcrumbs! There are two basic methods for making brown bread ice-cream: one calls for the breadcrumbs (which should be from an old-fashioned, nutty-textured wholemeal loaf as opposed to one of the soft wrapped variety) to be pre-soaked in rum, the other calls for the breadcrumbs to be toasted with sugar. The choice is yours.

Brown Bread Ice-Cream with Rum (or another tipple)

3 oz. (84 g.) brown breadcrumbs
2 tbs. rum
½ pint (280 ml.) double cream
1 egg white

Soak the breadcrumbs in the rum until all the liquor is absorbed. Whip the double cream and egg white until stiff and fold in the drunken crumbs. Turn into a freezer tray and semi-freeze. Scoop out into a bowl and stir to break down the ice chips. Pack into a tub and freeze until firm.

Vanilla Ice-Cream with Toasted Brown Breadcrumbs

vanilla ice-cream made with custard (see p.93)
3 tbs. brown breadcrumbs
2 tbs. brown sugar

Toast the brown breadcrumbs and sugar until both are even browner and stir into the vanilla ice-cream when it is taken from the freezer for its final stirring. Nice and sticky this, but an irresistible ice-cream evolves.

BUTTER

'To make this Butter, shee shall beat or cherne it a great while in Vessels made for this purpose.'
Surflet & Markham in *Maison rustique* (1616)

Butter is made by agitating cream with sufficient vigour to force the fat globules to first granulate and then mass together, leaving the watery liquid – the buttermilk – as a separate by-product. There are many ways of achieving this, ranging from the efficient, commercial machinery, to the pure simplicity, albeit arm-aching ritual, of shaking cream in a screw-topped jar. The latter process requires considerable enthusiasm and energy, as did the old-fashioned butter churns – a fact confirmed by Shakespeare's 'and bootlesse make the breathless huswife cherne'.

The making of butter has always incited a certain amount of magic and mystique. For instance, if the butter was slow to come it was said to have gone to 'sleep' and this inconvenience was blamed on an angry witch or bad tempered spirit! Various charms and customs were observed in order to try and counteract this unwelcome immortal meddling; a poker might be laid on top of the churn, or a boot perhaps tied to the bottom as lucky omens. And some incantation might be voiced –

Come, butter, come
Come, butter, come,
Peter stands at the gate
Waiting for a buttered cake,
Come, butter, come.

until the wretched butter did! Whilst butter can still be reckoned to have a mind of its own, the present-day butter churner does at least have more knowledge regarding the best temperature at which to coax the butter out of the cream.

You can make butter from either raw or pasteurized cream, or else from soured cream. The former is best for producing a creamy, unsalted butter, but does take longer to churn than the latter, which is usually thought to make better salted butter. Electric butter churns are available but it is hardly worth buying one unless you have a herd of cows, and are planning to make rather a lot of butter! An ordinary electric cake mixer or blender will make small amounts of butter without too much fuss, or else a hand butter churn – usually a glass jar affair with paddles – will yield butter with a little elbow grease.

To Make Creamy, Unsalted Butter

To make about 8 oz. (225 g.)
1 pint (560 ml.) double cream
3–4 tbs. cold water plus more cold water for washing butter

Do not attempt to economize by using a thinner cream – if you do, you will simply make less butter. Put the cream, at room temperature, into a blender, mixer, churn or whatever. If you are using a mixer and bowl, make sure it's a large bowl, otherwise the stuff will splutter gaily everywhere. Churn away, slowly at first and resting your machine at intervals if it is not a very robust affair, until the cream starts to 'break', i.e. go granular or bitty. Throw in the cold water. This is known as 'breaking water' and helps the process along. However, the total amount of breaking water should never be greater than a quarter of the cream used. Continue churning for another 30 seconds or so, until the butter clumps together and leaves some liquid – the buttermilk – separate. Pour off the buttermilk and keep it for drinking or cooking.

Now you have to wash the butter. Simply add a couple of cups of cold water to the bowl, mix around a bit, and pour the water off. Repeat the procedure until the water runs off completely clear. Turn the butter onto a wet board or plate. Now work the butter – knead it almost – to expel all final traces of the buttermilk which, if left in the butter, will cause it to go rancid. Ideally, 'scotch hands', rinsed with cold water to facilitate the operation, are employed for this. These are large, flat, wooden implements rather like unperforated spatulas. If unavailable, something else in the kitchen will suffice – a couple of large spoons for example.

When no more liquid can be coaxed out of the butter, shape it into a round or roll, or smooth it into a dish. A fashion for nostalgia has prompted the re-manufacture of various stamps and moulds, and these can be tracked down without too much bother. Wooden ones should be sterilized with boiling water and then plunged into ice cold water just prior to being pressed onto the butter – this helps to make a well defined pattern. This butter will have a pale, creamy colour with just a faint hint of yellow about it. The colour of butter, incidentally, is determined by the carotene found in grass and green vegetables. Hence, butter produced from cows that have been grazing on lush summer pastures will tend to be yellower than that produced from cows that have been forced to feed inside in the winter months.

To Make Salted Butter

To make about 8 oz. (225 g.)
1 pint (560 ml.) soured cream
3–4 tbs. cold water, plus extra for washing the butter
1–2 tsp. salt

The cream may be unpasteurized cream which has soured naturally, or else pasteurized cream which has been soured either commercially or at home. (A tablespoon of cultured buttermilk or natural yoghurt will sour pasteurized cream overnight if left in a warmish place.) However, do not be tempted to use pasteurized cream that has merely gone 'off'. This has been contaminated by unfavourable bacteria and butter produced from it will taste as bad as the undesirable cream itself. The method for making salted butter is exactly the same as the previous recipe, but, once the last traces of buttermilk have been expelled, work in salt to taste. Salted butter is not so good for cooking but it does keep longer. Many people prefer it – if the quantity of salted butter sold, as opposed to unsalted, is anything to go by.

fig. 2.
fig.

fig 3.

Butter in Haste

From Winter Cream, or from the Milk of One Cow (late 19th century)

'Take the milk fresh from the cow; strain it into clean pans. Set it over a gentle fire until it is scalding hot; do not let it boil. Then set it aside. When it is cold, skim off the cream; the milk will still be fit for any ordinary use. When you have a sufficient quantity of cream, put it in a clean earthen basin; beat it with a wooden spoon until the butter is made, which will not be long; then take it from the milk and work it with a little cold water. Put a small tablespoon of fine salt to each pound of butter and work it in; a small spoonful of fine white sugar worked in with the salt is also an improvement. Make the butter into a large roll, cover it with muslin, and keep it in a cool place.'

Buttermilk

'Of the making of Butter is left a kinde of whey, which they commonly call Butter milke, or soure milke.'
Thomas Cogan in *The haven of health* (1584)

As aforementioned, the buttermilk left from butter-making should not be allowed to gurgle down the drain, but should be kept for drinking (it is highly nutritious) or else designated for scone- or cake-baking in which it is very useful. Of course, if you used soured cream (raw or pasteurized) to make the butter, the buttermilk collected can be used as a starter, or ripener, for cheese-making, as it will have the necessary lactic-acid-producing bacteria present. However, if you used ordinary pasteurized cream (i.e. unsoured), the buttermilk will not be suitable as the majority of the lactic-acid-producing bacteria will have been destroyed by the pasteurizing process. You will note that cultured buttermilk is always called for when used as a starter to ripen milk for cheese-making.

To Make Cream from Butter

'He noticed the defendant driving a milk float towards him at a great speed.'
Bury Times (September 3rd, 1887)

After all the effort that goes into making butter from cream, it is amusing to learn that many people frequently reverse the process. This is not so mad as it sounds – especially at times when butter is government subsidized which means cream made from butter is considerably cheaper than that bought from the milkman. Hand-operated devices for this devilish practice are available commercially (see Cream-making machines in Glossary) as are various attachments for certain electric mixers. One maker's recipe for a basic cream reads as follows.

To make 10 oz. (280 **g.**) (½ **pint**)
Put 5 oz. (140 g.) pasteurized milk in a saucepan with 5 oz. (140 g.) chopped unsalted butter. Heat slowly to melt the butter (do not let the milk boil). Pour the hot mixture into the cup and pump through the Cream Maker into the base unit. Stir the mixture, then put in a cool place or refrigerator until it is cold and ready to serve. The mixture will thicken as it cools.

To de-salt butter
Put 4 oz. (112 g.) butter in a pan with 1 pint (560 ml.) water and bring to the boil for 2–3 minutes. Leave to cool until the butter forms a crust on top of the water. Remove the butter which is now unsalted.

YOGHURT

'The yahourt-merchant, with his . . . trays covered with little brown clay basins, showing forth the creamy whiteness of his merchandise.'

Pardoe in *City of Sultan* (1838)

Yoghurt can be made from milk that has been treated in virtually any way – skimmed, pasteurized, dried, tinned, etc. However, the most suitable milk for yoghurt-making is either sterilized or U.H.T. as it has already been heated to a temperature high enough to kill off any undesirable bacteria. If ordinary pasteurized milk is used, it should first be brought to the boil and simmered for 2–3 minutes. It must, of course, be cooled to the temperature stipulated in the recipe, before the yoghurt culture is introduced. If this is not done, the heat will kill off the culture, and there will be no bacteria left to thicken the milk.

To make 2 pints (1.120 lit.)
2 pints (1.120 lit.) U.H.T. or sterilized milk
1–2 tbs. natural yoghurt

Put the milk in a pan and heat to 110°F/43°C. Remove from the stove and stir in the natural yoghurt. The next operation depends on the equipment to hand, but the idea is to maintain the mixture at a constant temperature until it thickens to the desired consistency – 8 hours or so. Commercial yoghurt-makers are widely available but the same results can be obtained by following any one of these methods:

(1) Transfer the warm milk and starter to a bowl. Cover it and leave it in a warm place. An airing cupboard kept at a constant temperature is generally a suitable venue if not too chock-a-block with sheets, etc.

(2) Transfer the mixture either to an insulated flask or wide-necked vacuum flask, pre-heated with hot water (check the capacity first of course!). Alternatively, a smaller quantity of yoghurt – half this recipe – can be made, and an insulated ice-bucket employed. If the bucket has water drainage holes in the bottom (but many do not), line it with foil first.

(3) Leave the mixture in the pan, cover and wrap the whole thing in a blanket or old eiderdown – very clumsy but quite effective.

When the yoghurt is ready, turn it into a bowl and whisk it lightly to make a really smooth, creamy yoghurt. Store in the refrigerator until required. Remember to save a couple of tablespoons of yoghurt to make the next batch.

Flavouring and Sweetening Yoghurt

Yoghurt can be flavoured and sweetened in numerous ways. Chopped fresh or tinned fruits, berries, dried fruits, ground nuts, sesame seeds, jams, honey, golden syrup, treacle and so on can be blended into yoghurt to ring the changes. Mixed with chopped chives, yoghurt makes a mild oniony salad dressing, and yoghurt-coated cucumber cubes are good, as a side dish – a raita – for calming down a hot, spicy curry.

Cooking with Yoghurt

When yoghurt is cooked for a brief spell only – added, for instance, to thicken a soup just prior to serving – there is no problem, but when subjected to several hours cooking, yoghurt invariably separates. Hence it is advisable to stabilize yoghurt before you cook it for any length of time.

To Stabilize Yoghurt

1 pint (560 ml.) natural yoghurt
½ tbs. cornflour
1 tbs. milk

Blend the cornflour with the milk to make a paste. Mix into the yoghurt in a pan. Put the pan over a moderate heat and, stirring deliberately in one direction only, i.e. clockwise or otherwise, bring to the boil. Turn down the ring and leave to simmer, without further stirring and without a lid – very important this – until it thickens. This will take 5 or 6 minutes. Once thickened, the yoghurt can be safely cooked without fear of a curdled disaster resulting.

Baked Yoghurt Custard

$\frac{1}{4}$ pint (140 ml.) milk
$\frac{1}{2}$ pint (280 ml.) stabilized yoghurt
2 large eggs
1–2 tbs. vanilla sugar (or ordinary sugar with a few drops of vanilla essence)
nutmeg
butter

Butter either a one-pint oven dish or four individual ramekins. Mix the milk and yoghurt together. Beat the eggs with the vanilla sugar, and then beat in the milk and yoghurt. Pour the mixture into the prepared dish or ramekins and stand in a tin of warm water. Sprinkle with ground nutmeg and bake at 350°F or Gas mark 4 for about 30 minutes, or until set. Serve straight away, drizzled with honey if liked.

JUNKET

Junket

'The seede . . . is often used in comfits, or served at the table with other junketting dishes.'

Gerarde in his *Herbal* (1597)

'The good woman . . . was in such a hurry to junket her neighbours.'

H. Walpole (1745)

In days gone by, 'to junket', or 'to go a-junketing', meant to feast, to entertain or to engage in some sort of frivolity. Nowadays, alas, junket is more likely to be regarded as a rather bland milk dessert. But bland it need not be. The following recipe, of Devonshire origin, is quite delectable, and looks quite festive dished up in a pretty china bowl.

To make 1 pint
1 pint (560 ml.) milk (not U.H.T. or sterilized)
1–2 level tbs. sugar
1 tbs. brandy
1 tsp. junket rennet or 1 tablet
clotted or whipped cream
cinnamon or nutmeg

Gently heat the milk to 98°F/37°C (i.e. blood heat), and remove from the stove. Stir in the sugar, brandy and rennet, and pour into a china bowl. Leave, undisturbed, until set – the exact time depends on the brand of rennet, room temperature, etc., but some junkets set in 15 minutes. Just prior to serving, smother with cream and spice with cinnamon or nutmeg.

Epilogue

To make Milk Punch that will keep for Years, and go to the Indies good (and fit for any dairymaid!)

'Take six quarts of Brandy, put to it the Peel of twenty Lemons, the Peel of four Seville Oranges, put it into the Brandy to steep four and twenty hours, then put to your Brandy two quarts of lemon and orange juice, almost Three Pints of Seville Orange Juice, Five Quarts of Water, Four large Nutmegs grated, and put two pounds and a half of double refined sugar, let these stand one day and Night and then boil three quarts and a Pint of Milk, when it boils put it to your Brandy, let it stand all Night; the Next Morning run it thro' a Jelly Bag, till it is clear as Rock-water.'

Hannah Glasse in *The Servant's Directory or House-keeper's Companion* (MDCCLX)

Glossary

Annatto
A harmless preparation obtained from the seeds of *Bixa orellanna*, traditionally used to colour some cheeses and butters a fiery orange. Do not be tempted to substitute an artifical colouring – such have been known to change milk products to strange shades of purple as they mature! It may be obtained from: Chr. Hansen's Laboratory Ltd., 476 Basingstoke Rd, Reading RG2 OQL. They also sell dairy cultures (e.g. *Lactobacillus bulgarius* for yoghurt), rennet, etc., by mail order.

Ass's milk

'If the Ass's Milk stand twelve Hours, it will gather no cream.'
Nicholas Robinson (1725)

The above mentioned is caused by the very low fat content found in ass's milk. Thus donkeys cannot be relied upon to supply milk to make rich creamy cheeses but, if Cleopatra is to be believed, their milk is excellent for bathing in.

Buffalo's milk
This has three times as much butter fat as cow's milk and is traditionally used to make the creamy Italian cheese, Mozzarella.

Buttermilk
Buttermilk is the liquid left when cream is churned to make butter. When butter is made from raw cream (full of lactic-acid-producing bacteria), the buttermilk that is collected retains its natural bacteria. Left to its own devices, this bacteria will reproduce and consequently thicken the buttermilk, variably, according to the time it is left and the temperature of the environs. Alternatively, when pasteurized cream is used to make a fresh butter, the resultant buttermilk too is pasteurized, and somewhat flavourless. So, to re-introduce a tangy flavour, most buttermilk has a bacteria culture added and is sold as cultured buttermilk.

Channel Islands milk
Milk from the much prized Jersey and Guernsey cows has a higher butter fat content than ordinary milk, and makes rich, creamy cheeses. It is easily distinguishable by its very definite, yellow cream line.

Cheese cultures
Diary cultures for yoghurt, cheese, sour cream, etc., can be obtained from: Culture Magic (U.K.) Ltd, 82 Murillo Rd, London SE13.

Cheese-making equipment
Several firms sell cheese mats, moulds, etc. Two reputable firms who issue catalogues and deal with postal enquiries are: Small Scale Supplies, Widdington, Saffron Walden, Essex; (telephone: Saffron Walden (0799) 40922), who sell two-tiered moulds used for Coulommier cheese.
Self-sufficiency and Smallholding Supplies, The Old Palace, Priory Road, Wells, Somerset.

Cheese vat
A large container which is employed to contain the milk in several stages of cheese-making whenever large quantities of milk are used. A stainless steel pan with, obviously, a capacity sufficient to hold the milk needed for the cheese being made makes a perfect cheese vat. Failing the acquisition of this rather expensive ideal, various enamelled pans can suffice. I have been advised that iron, copper or any other un-enamelled metal should not be used because of the risk of a chemical reaction. In some recipes, a white plastic dairy bucket serves as an admirable cheese vat. This type of bucket will withstand quite high temperatures (but do check when you buy it!) and can be stood, with the milk to be heated, in a sink of hot water. The milk is then stirred, to distribute the heat, until the requisite temperature is attained.

Cream-making machines
Hand-operated machines available commercially from Arlington Food and Arts, 49 Formans Road, Sparkhill, Birmingham.

Dairy thermometer
This is preferable to an ordinary sugar thermometer as it will float on the milk's surface.

Ewe's milk

'Oh! what wonderful dishes Chambertin and Roquefort are to restore love, and also to bring to maturity a growing love.'
Casanova (1757)

Although ewe's (or sheep's) milk is used to make a number of celebrated cheeses – the French, blue-veined Roquefort, the Portuguese Queijo de Serra, and the Greek *feta* for instance – ewe's milk cheeses are somewhat rare aliments these days. They are invariably veined, pickled or heavily salted to inject extra pungency. Very little ewe's milk cheese is made in England nowadays, and even abroad, ewe's milk and goat's milk are often erroneously regarded as the same thing, with cheese recipes vaguely calling for one or the other, or a mixture of both to be used. Theoretically though it should be remembered that ewe's milk has both a higher butter fat and protein content than either goat's or cow's milk.

Goat's milk

'Dr Gregory . . . advises the Highland air, and the use of goat milk whey.'
Smollett in *The Expedition of Humphrey Clinker* (1771)

Goat's milk makes a slightly softer cheese than cow's milk. This is due to its natural homogenized structure – the same factor which makes goat's milk such an easily digested food for invalids. Its actual composition, though, is similar to cow's milk, and cheeses made from the two kinds of milk do not taste all that different when eaten fresh. However, as it ripens, goat's milk cheese acquires a distinct, peppery-hot pungency. Goat's milk is fairly easy to buy in Britain and can be used, in place of cow's milk, to make most of the cheeses in this book. However, it should be rennetted at a slightly lower temperature – about 5° F/3° C less.

Homogenized milk
Warm milk is forced through tiny holes to break down the fat globules in the milk. Once broken, these small particles remain evenly distributed throughout the milk, and thus no cream line forms. The milk is then subjected to the same heat treatment as ordinary pasteurized milk. The disintegration of the fat globules does make the milk more easily digested but also makes it unsuitable for cheese-making.

Lactic acid
This forms naturally in milk as it sours but the formation is arrested by pasteurization. Lactic acid can be bought in bottles, from Boots and the like, and can be used to re-activate the souring process.

Pasteurized milk
Practically all milk currently sold to the public is pasteurized to destroy undesirable bacteria. Ordinary pasteurized milk is subjected to mild heat treatment – 161° F/71.7° C for at least 15 seconds, and then rapidly cooled to not more than 50° F/10° C.

Rennet
This is a preparation made from the stomach of an unweaned calf, but enzymes with similar coagulation abilities may be extracted from some plants. Junket rennet will make cheeses which require a very soft curd, but normally it is necessary to use a proper cheese rennet. It is usually mixed with boiled and cooled water – 6 parts to 1 part rennet – to facilitate mixing with the milk.

Starter
A bacterial culture, introduced in the early stages of cheese-making, to change the milk sugar (lactose) into lactic acid, and also to flavour the cheese in some cases. Commercial cheese starters are available but quite expensive. Natural yoghurt or cultured buttermilk are much cheaper, more easily available, and produce similar results.

Sterilized milk
This kind of milk is homogenized, bottled and sealed, and then subjected to a much higher temperature than pasteurized milk – not less that 212° F/100° C for 20–30 minutes – and then cooled. Not suitable for cheese-making but good for yoghurt-making.

U.H.T. Milk (Ultra Heat Treated Milk)
This milk is first homogenized and then subjected to ultra high temperatures – not less than 270° F/132.2° C for one second. It is aseptically packed in foil-lined containers in which it will keep wholesome for several months until opened. Not suitable for cheese but good for yoghurt.

Bibliography

Axler, Bruce H., *The Cheese Handbook* (Cassell, London, 1970)

Bowdage, A., *Practical Hints on Dairy Work and Management* (1894)

Cheke, Val, *The Story of Cheese-making in Britain* (Routledge and Kegan Paul, London 1959)

Christian, Glynn, *Cheese and Cheese-making* (Macdonald, London, 1977)

Cooper, Michael, *Discovering Farmhouse Cheese* (Shire Publications, Aylesbury, 1978)

Davis, J.G., *A Dictionary of Dairying* (Leonard Hill, London, 1955)

Fraser, Shelagh, *The Cheeses of Old England*

Hartley, D., *Food in England* (Macdonald, London, 1954)

Hutchinson, Peggy, *Old English Cookery* (W. Foulsham & Co Ltd, Slough, 1973)

Layton, T.A., *The Cheese Handbook* (Dover Publications, U.S.A., 1973)

Murray, Ross (ed.), *The Modern Householder* (1872)

Ogilvy, Susan, *Making Cheeses* (Batsford, London, 1976)

Pike, Mary Ann, *Town and Country Fare and Fable* (David & Charles, Newton Abbot, 1978)

Sheldon, J.P., *Dairy Farming* (1890)

Singer, Andrew and Len Street, *Backyard Dairybook* (Prism Press, Dorset, 1978)

Soyer, Alexis, *The Pantropheon* (1853)

Stone, Helen, *Churns and Cheeses* (National Dairy Council Publication)

Thear, Katie, *The Home Dairying Book* (Broad Leys Publishing, 1978)

Tisdale and Robinson, *Buttermaking on the Farm and at the Creamery* (1907)

Tisdale and Robinson, *The Practice of Soft Cheesemaking* (1908)

Twamley, Josiah, *Dairying Exemplified* (1784)

Yeld, Ellen, M.B.E., *Practical Cheese-making* (Orphans Printing Press, 1919)